# BUILDERS OF CATHOLIC AMERICA

## Albert J. Nevins M.M.

Our Sunday Visitor Publishing
Huntington, Indiana 46750

International Standard Book Number: 0-87973-582-1
Library of Congress Catalog Card Number: 85-72363

*Cover design and illustrations by James E. McIlrath*

PRINTED IN THE UNITED STATES OF AMERICA

# Contents

# Contents

Part One / The Blackrobes □ INTRODUCTION ............. 1

   1 • **New York Martyr**
      *Isaac Jogues* ............................... 3

   2 • **The Mississippi Explorer**
      *Jacques Marquette* ..................... 14

   3 • **The Missouri Traveler**
      *Pierre Jean De Smet* ................... 27

Part Two / The Pioneers □ INTRODUCTION ........... 41

   4 • **The First Family**
      *The Carrolls* ............................. 43

   5 • **Father of California**
      *Junípero Serra* .......................... 68

   6 • **Tarheel Apostle**
      *Thomas Frederick Price* ............. 89

Part Three / The Emigrés □ INTRODUCTION ........ 107

   7 • **Our First Priest**
      *Stephen Badin* ......................... 110

   8 • **The Forgotten Bishop**
      *John Dubois* ............................ 118

9 • Bishop on Horseback
*Simon Bruté* ................................. 137

10 • The Mountain Man
*Joseph Machebeuf* ............................ 148

**Part Four / The Irish Brigade** ☐ INTRODUCTION ... 167
11 • Peer of Prelates
*John England* ................................. 168

12 • The American Cardinal
*James Gibbons* .............................. 183

**Part Five / The Women** ☐ INTRODUCTION .......... 207
13 • The Bridge
*Elizabeth Ann Seton* ......................... 209

14 • Sanctity on the Frontier
*Rose Philippine Duchesne* .................... 218

15 • Citizen Saint
*Frances Xavier Cabrini* ...................... 225

16 • A Woman of Conscience
*Dorothy Day* ................................. 237

**Index of People** ................................. 251

# *PART ONE*

## The Blackrobes □ *INTRODUCTION*

If the blood of martyrs — to paraphrase Tertullian — is the seed of Christianity, the soil of North America has been liberally sown. From the time of Father Juan de Padilla (who, instead of leaving Kansas with the Coronado expedition, stayed to work among the Indians of central Kansas only to find martyrdom there in 1542) to modern-day times (when, in 1985, for example, Father John Rossiter was murdered as he knelt in prayer before his church altar in Onalaska, Wisconsin), men and women have died for their faith in Christ and His Church.

In the long list of American martyrs two groups stand out — the Franciscans and the Jesuits. The former mostly died in the Southwest, and the latter in the Northeast. It was the Jesuits who gave the United States its first saints — René Goupil (who died in 1642) and Isaac Jogues and John Lalande (who followed in 1646). These three — along with fellow Jesuits Anthony Daniel, John de Brébeuf, Gabriel Lalemant, Charles Garnier, and Noël Chabanel — were canonized in 1930.

The Jesuits were a unique group. They had gone to New France at the behest of Cardinal Richelieu, chief minister of France, to Christianize the Indians. Each missioner had the obligation to make regular written reports of his work to his Jesuit superior. These reports were sent back to France where they were published as the *Jesuit Relations*. The diaries were popular reading, not only for their geography and anthropology, but because they revealed in understatement the human suffering that went into missionary work. The *Relations* are still the best source of knowledge about Indian life and customs as they existed before European settlement changed them.

The Jesuits were known to the Indians as "Black-robes" because of the black soutanes they wore. To illustrate the contribution these intrepid men made to the development of the Catholic Church in the United States, three representative figures have been chosen: Isaac Jogues, Jacques Marquette, and Pierre Jean De Smet.

# CHAPTER 1

## New York Martyr

### Isaac Jogues

"I shall not return" was the prophecy Isaac Jogues made to a friend as this mutilated and torture-scarred man left Quebec for his last journey to the Iroquois Indians of what is now upper New York state. That a man who had not only seen his companions savagely killed but who had suffered so much personally should willingly return to his tormentors is hard for the modern mind to grasp. But such a man was Jogues.

Isaac Jogues was born on January 10, 1607, to a prominent family of Orléans, France. As a youth he studied in a Jesuit school where he admired the black-cassocked professors who belonged to a young society which had already earned a great reputation throughout Europe for its dedication to the work of the Church. Men like Francis Xavier (who had died a lonely death on an outpost in the China Sea) and Paul Miki (who had been crucified in distant Japan) captured his youthful imagination.

When he was seventeen, Jogues told his mother that he wished to become a priest. At first his mother was overjoyed. The connections of her family and those of her husband could prove useful to her son's advancement in the Church. But her joy was short-lived when her son explained that he did not want to be a priest in France. He wanted to become a Jesuit and leave France for some mission. Madame Jogues tried to talk her son out of his hopes; failing, she gave her permission.

When young Jogues applied to the Society of Jesus, he was asked why he wanted to join the society.

"I want to be a missioner, to go to Ethiopia and die there," the boy replied.

"No, you will go to New France to die," responded the admissions officer.

Although a diligent student, Jogues did not find seminary studies easy. It was a great relief to him that because of the urgent need for priests in New France, he was ordained in January 1636, a year early. He returned to Orléans for his first solemn high Mass and then after a thirty-day retreat found himself along with three companion-missioners awaiting a storm-delayed sailing in Dieppe. On April 8 the weather cleared and the ships took off for the New World, a two-month journey.

On the morning of June 2, Father Jogues stepped ashore on St. Louis de Miscou Island, near the Gaspé Peninsula. He found two Jesuits there, men who had studied with him in France. "I have entered Paradise," he wrote his mother in a letter that the ship would carry back to France, in a spirit based more on his zeal than on his poor surroundings. It was exactly a month later when he finally reached his first goal, the steep bluff at Quebec where the Jesuits had two houses. But he was not to stay there long. He was moved on to Three Rivers, or Trois Rivières, also a Jesuit headquarters. (Three Rivers is a town named after the three channels through which the St. Maurice River empties into the St. Lawrence River.) Here he was told to wait for Huron Indians who would escort him to his mission post at Ihonatiria on Georgian Bay — a three-week

4

journey to this outpost of Lake Huron that would involve seemingly endless paddling, frequent backbreaking portages, and monotonous meals of corn mush.

So the weeks and months passed. Jogues became proficient in the Huron language, preached, converted, and baptized. During this period he made two long journeys — one to the Niagara River, near present-day Buffalo, to the edge of Iroquois territory, and another to the area of Sault Ste. Marie, reporting each time there were souls to be gained with more missioners.

In June of 1642, Jogues was sent on the thirty-five-day journey to Three Rivers for supplies, also visiting Quebec, where he found René Goupil, who would go back to Georgian Bay with him as a lay missioner. They went back to Three Rivers, organized their supplies, were joined by William Couture, another lay worker, and on August 1, despite rumors of marauding Mohawks (one of the tribes making up the Iroquois confederacy), set out in a flotilla of twelve canoes whose occupants included three Frenchmen, about forty Huron braves returning home, and a Christian Huron girl named Theresa. The first day passed uneventfully, but unknowingly they were being watched by Mohawks. The next day, shortly after daybreak, when they had started out anew, the Mohawk trap was sprung. The seven rear canoes were able to paddle away and escape, but the forward five with the Frenchmen and the girl were cut off. These canoes headed for shore and the safety of the forest, but other Mohawks were waiting there.

In the melee that followed, Jogues, Couture, and the girl escaped into the underbrush. The Hurons were quickly overcome. Jogues from his place of concealment saw

Theresa being dragged back to the group. The Mohawks were raining blows on the captives. Jogues realized that he could not allow Goupil and the others to be taken to torture and possible death alone. As a priest, he had to be with them. He came forth from his hiding place and the enemy fell upon him, striking him and ripping off his soutane. Meanwhile, Couture had been brought in. He also had given himself up to be with his friends.

The Mohawks and their captives set out for the long journey south. It took five days to reach Lake Champlain where, on an island, there was a large band of Mohawk warriors encamped. The prisoners were made to run the gauntlet where they were beaten, branded, and burned. At last, after many days, the war party and its captives reached the Mohawk village of Ossernenon, located on the Mohawk River, just west of what is now Albany. Here the captives again ran the gauntlet, stumbling up a hill while being beaten with clubs, sticks, and whips. The captives were tied up, and Mohawk women gnawed at Jogues's fingers. His thumb was cut off, as was that of Goupil. The prisoners were divided up among various Mohawk villages; Jogues and Goupil were to remain in Ossernenon.

Jogues and Goupil were turned over to the keeping of the head of a longhouse. The Indian did not like them and treated them as slaves, lower than women. They had to work in the fields, haul water, and take only leavings of food. One day Goupil instinctively made the sign of the cross over a sick baby. He was seen by two young braves. He realized he had been imprudent and went to find Jogues. He located him in a ravine behind the village where the priest often went to pray. He told the Jesuit

what he had done. The two men began to pray the rosary when the two braves stepped out from the trees. One of the Indians grasped Goupil and forced him to his knees while the other smashed a tomahawk against the Frenchman's head. Jogues recited the words of absolution. The braves forced Jogues to return to the village. The next day he found Goupil's body on a garbage heap and hid it until it could be given proper burial; but when he returned to bury it, it was gone and he never did find it.

As a result of the murder, Jogues was .transferred from the longhouse where he had been living into the care of an old Indian woman, daughter of a chief, wife of a chief, and mother of a chief. She was a respected woman who even sat on Mohawk councils. She treated Jogues with kindness, calling him "Nephew," while he referred to her as "Aunt." She gave Jogues a copy of *The Imitation of Christ* which had been among the booty taken in his capture. He was overjoyed at the gift. Jogues was also sent out by Aunt on hunting and fishing parties.

It was in returning from one such fishing party that Jogues escaped. The Mohawks had taken him to the Hudson River, south of the Dutch trading post of Fort Orange at the town of Rensselaerswyck (now Albany). Outside the town a Dutch settler, married to a Mohawk woman, had a farm, and passing Mohawks were allowed to sleep in his barn. Here Jogues and two Indians retired for the night before traveling to Ossernenon the following day. During the night, when the Indians were asleep, he escaped. The Dutch hid him and moved him from hiding place to hiding place while the angry Mohawks searched for him. He was finally smuggled aboard a Dutch vessel and in this way made his way down the river to New Amsterdam (present-day New York), where he was welcomed and feted by the Protestant Dutch. In November 1643, one of the last ships to sail before winter set in carried him across the Atlantic. In the Bay of Falmouth he was transferred to a Dutch coastal boat, and on Christmas Day he was put ashore on the Breton coast where he found a small church, heard Mass, and at last received the body of his Lord.

Jogues's return to France caused something of a sensation. He had been given up for dead and his "resurrection" alone was enough to make him a celebrity. But his mangled hands were proof of the tortures he had endured and everyone wanted to meet him, to hear him talk about New France and the Jesuits there. He was troubled that he could not offer Mass because Church law demanded the use of thumb and index fingers. The superior general of the Jesuits and the queen of France each petitioned Pope Urban VIII for a dispensation. The pope replied: "It would be shameful that a martyr of Christ not be allowed to drink the blood of Christ." Thus Father Jogues was restored to the altar, and a two-year emptiness was ended.

After visiting his mother and family, Jogues went to Paris. He wanted to return to New France, but his superiors were divided about letting him go back. They felt he faced certain death if he was recaptured by the Mohawks, and there were those who thought he could do more for the Society of Jesus lecturing around the country. Finally, the decision was left up to him. It was not a difficult one for him to make, and in the spring of 1644 he sailed aboard a troopship for his chosen field of labor.

Jogues was sent to work at Montreal. He could not go further west because the Iroquois were raiding the northern tribes. The Hurons had been badly decimated, and the Algonquins were also suffering attacks. The new French governor, Charles de Montmagny, who had arrived in the convoy carrying Jogues, was determined to make peace. That summer of 1644 he began sending out peace feelers. In July and September of the following year the Iroquois met with the French, and an uneasy truce began to take shape. Montmagny promised he would send an ambassador to the Iroquois in the spring of the next year.

When the choice was made for an emissary, the governor selected Jogues. The Blackrobe had lived with the Mohawks, knew their language and customs, and saw his field of labor in the tribes of the future state of New York. Jogues was delighted to be chosen, and on May 16, 1646, two Mohawk canoes left Three Rivers with Jogues, Jean Bordon (a French cartographer, or map-maker), two Algonquin braves who were to be ambassadors from their tribe, and a Mohawk escort. Jogues was dressed in lay clothes, since in this case he was representing the secular state. He did, however, carry a box with him containing his soutane and Mass necessities.

Although the trip was full of bitter memories — spots where he had been abused and tortured — Jogues gave no sign of dwelling on past offenses. The party made its way down Lake Champlain and then into another lake that was on no French map. Bordon sketched it in for future explorers and Jogues named it "Lake of the Blessed Sacrament." Later the English would change the name to honor their own king, calling it Lake George, the name which it has today. On June 4, the party reached Rensselaerswyck, where Jogues paused to give thanks to those who had helped him escape. Then the group moved west along the

Mohawk River to Ossernenon, where the first person he went to see was Aunt. He left his Mass box with her.

The next day he went to Tionontoguen, where the Iroquois chiefs had gathered. A council meeting was held, and the chiefs declared their friendship for the French and Christians and their acceptance of the peace treaty. Jogues was uneasy in that no chief had mentioned the Hurons and Algonquins who were supposed to be part of the treaty. When the council ended, Jogues approached an Ossernenon chief whom he knew and asked why the northern tribes had not been mentioned. He was told that the Iroquois were at peace with the Christian Hurons and Algonquins but not the rest. He learned that Seneca and Oneida braves were already heading for Huron country and he knew it was impossible for them to tell the difference between a Christian Huron and a pagan Huron. He realized that the peace treaty worked out in Montreal was not going to mean much. He decided that he had better return to Quebec and report to the governor. The pagan Algonquins and Hurons would believe that the French had sacrificed them for the Christians and it could do great harm for future work among them.

Jogues explained his findings to the governor and it was agreed that he not return immediately to the Mohawks. In September a delegation of Huron chiefs, angered at violations of the peace treaty, arrived to discuss retaliation with the governor. He persuaded them to send a new ambassador to the Iroquois and asked Father Jogues to accompany him. The priest said he would go — but as a missioner, not a French representative — and that he would remain among the Mohawks and try to convert them. The new delegation set out on September 24. Jogues took along John Lalande, a young lay worker, as companion and assistant, and Otrihoure, the Huron ambassador, was accompanied by two Huron braves, who were to desert the party because of their fear of the enemy.

After twenty days of hard travel and portages the two Frenchmen and the Huron were almost within sight of Ossernenon when a screaming Mohawk band rushed out of the woods and overcame them. They were beaten and marched into Ossernenon. Jogues and his companions were allowed to go to Aunt's house where he learned that his Mass kit had been thrown into the river. That summer had been one of drought, crop failure, and sickness. The Indians blamed their troubles on evil spirits in the box. The next day the Indian leaders went to Tionontoguen to discuss the Blackrobe's capture with the other chiefs. However, some braves decided that they would not wait for a decision. Jogues was called outside Aunt's house where he was tomahawked and decapitated. His head was placed on a sharp pole of the palisade, and the boys of the village dragged his body through the camp so that it could be kicked. When they tired of this pastime, they threw the remains in the river. Later, young Lalande went looking for the body, but he too was tomahawked and his head joined that of Jogues on the palisade. Otrihoure was to die some days later.

Jogues's death ended all attempts at peace. The Iroquois nation flooded north, west, and south. The Algonquins and the Hurons were decimated. The Erie, Illinois, Delaware, and Tuscarora tribes fell to Iroquois power. The Iroquois — consisting of the Mohawk, Onondaga, Oneida, Cayuga, and Seneca tribes — raided Catholic missions and put to death other Blackrobes they captured. By the time of the American Revolution, they were the dominant Indians in the northeastern United States. They sided with the British in the American War of Independence, and this was the beginning of the end of them as a mighty nation.

On January 20, 1930, Pope Pius XI raised Jogues and seven of his missionary companions to be saints of the Catholic Church. Ossernenon, where Jogues, Goupil, and Lalande died, is now the site of the National Shrine to the North American Martyrs. It has been renamed Auriesville, and each year thousands of tourists leave the New York State Thruway to walk the hilltop and visit the ravine where martyrs' blood made fertile the soil of a great nation.

# CHAPTER 2

## *The Mississippi Explorer*

### *Jacques Marquette*

It is one of the simplicities of geographers that the label of discoverer is given to people who were not the first ones there. Thus Christopher Columbus is called the discoverer of America, although there is ample evidence that Viking and Irish seafarers made landfall in North America long years before. Even they were not the first, since the Indians were already waiting. Perhaps the title belongs to that aborigine who first led a tribe across the land bridge that existed between Siberia and Alaska and thus began to people a continent. Then again perhaps not, since some off-course canoe might have landed earlier.

Thus it is with the Mississippi. This vast river — which, with its tributaries, was so essential to the opening of the United States — was certainly known by Indians. Álvar Núñez Cabeza de Vaca, in recounting his incredible journey across the breadth of America, wrote of it in his adventurous journal. Hernando de Soto found his grave in its waters. The Spanish named the mighty stream "River of the Holy Spirit." French voyageurs trapped fur-bearing animals in its upper reaches. Why then is Father Jacques Marquette called its discoverer when so many had been there ahead of him?

In this sense the French word for discovery is more exact than the English. The English word implies finding something for the first time, while the French *découvrir* means more to reveal, expose, or lay bare. In this basic meaning Columbus was the discoverer of America because he demonstrated a practical route to the New World, described some of its features, and spurred succeeding Spanish, French, Portuguese, and English expeditions. So Marquette can be called the discoverer of the Mississippi, since his journal revealed the river bisected the continent, running from north to south, and its tributaries opened up its vast interior. The exploration of Marquette and Louis Jolliet was enough to set imaginations afire with the great possibilities and potential that existed because waterways existed — the Illinois, Missouri, Ohio, Arkansas, and many lesser streams. It is one thing to indicate that something is there and quite another to show how it can be used.

It is also argued whether Marquette or Jolliet should get the credit. This matter did not seem to worry the two men concerned, since neither made claims; but over the years each man has developed a following. Advocates of the layman Jolliet suggest a Jesuit public-relations job put the priest Marquette in the discovery seat when in reality it was the practical woodsman's knowledge of Jolliet that made success possible. Jolliet, they point out, was a veteran of forest and river, a natural leader. Supporters of Marquette argue that it was his maps and journal that perpetuated the discoveries; they point out that Marquette was an educated man, while Jolliet was a diamond in the rough. Moreover, Marquette's backers claim, it was French custom to give Blackrobes responsibility, assigning laymen to assist them, and that therefore Marquette was the leader of the expedition and Jolliet only his helper. In any case, there is no evidence of rivalry between the two men. They worked together as companions and cooperators. Certainly, there is enough credit to be shared, and the question of who was the leader is irrelevant to the discoveries they made together.

Jacques Marquette was born on June 10, 1637, in Laon, France. Marquette's family was prominent and his mother was related to St. John Baptist de la Salle. He attended a Jesuit school and like other boys of his age was moved by accounts of Jesuit missionary activity in New France that appeared as the *Jesuit Relations*. At the age of seventeen he decided to join the Society of Jesus and this was followed by a dozen years of scholastic work as novice, priest, teacher. He was twenty-nine when he was assigned to New France, the *Relations* accounts making him fully aware of the difficulties that lay ahead.

On September 20, 1666, Jacques Marquette arrived at Quebec where the French were building a settlement. Besides the Jesuit house, there was a church, a hospital, an Ursuline convent, a barracks, and a warehouse which doubled as a theater. It was a far cry from the civilities of France, but Marquette was to remain there only three weeks before being sent on to the outpost at Three Rivers to study the Montagnais Indian language, an exasperating tongue which had many ways to say the same thing. In three years he not only learned Montagnais but six other dialects. In 1669 he was assigned to work among the Ottawas at Sault Ste. Marie, the last mission west in New France, ten weeks away by canoe and portages along rivers because the Iroquois made the lakes dangerous. Sault Ste. Marie had been founded years earlier as the base for French trade in western pelts. It was a center where Indians of various tribes came to bring their furs in trade for

French goods. It was here that Marquette first heard of a great river variously called Messipi, Mitchisisipi, and Misisipi (literally, "big river"). The Illinois Indians seemed to know most about this river, so Marquette learned the Illinois language.

In 1672 Marquette was at St. Ignace, a new outpost at the Straits of Mackinac, where Lake Michigan and Lake Huron joined. He built a chapel there to serve Huron converts. He wrote a long letter to a priestly confrere, telling of his hopes and disappointments, the main disappointment being that of backsliding converts. In the letter he describes woods "full of bears, stags, beavers, and wildcats." Food is plentiful and the annual harvest ample, he goes on to say. He regrets not having a bell for his chapel, he continues; and when he wants his converts for services, he has to go into the fields to call them. He mentions the copper deposits of the region. He sums up his work by concluding that "one needs the grace of perseverance."

Meanwhile, back in Quebec, an old dream of finding a water passage to the Western Sea (the Pacific) was still alive. The rumors of "the great river" that came from the frontier raised hope that this might be the way. The French governor — Louis de Buade, Comte de Palluau et de Frontenac — concluded that the rumors should be explored. Why Father Marquette was selected for the expedition is not known. Certainly Frontenac consulted with the Jesuit superior in New France. Marquette had a reputation for a singleness of purpose at least, if not for a strong constitution. He had become skilled in Indian ways and tongues. The rumors of the great river that he had heard from the tribes made him as knowledgeable as any. Moreover, he was already on the frontier and with Indians who could be used as guides. His openness and friendliness would be useful qualities in meeting unknown tribes.

At any rate, an entry in Marquette's journal, dated December 8, 1672, records the mission this way: "Monsieur Jollyet arrived with orders from Monsieur the Count de Frontenac, governor of New France, and Monsieur Talon, our intendant [a government official], bidding him to accomplish this discovery with me." An accompanying letter was from the Jesuit superior authorizing the priest to set out on this extraordinary journey. The same superior writing to his headquarters in France justified his selection of Marquette: "He has both tact and prudence, which are the chief characteristics required for the success of a voyage as dangerous as it is difficult. He has the courage to dread nothing where everything is to be feared."

Louis Jolliet, who suddenly appeared with the letter, was not unknown to Marquette. The two men had met a number of times and respected each other. Jolliet was twenty-seven years of age at this time and Marquette thirty-five. Jolliet had been born in New France, the son of a wagonmaker. He had attended a Jesuit school in Quebec but soon became a man of the wilderness, acting as trapper, guide, interpreter, and trader. He had proven himself bold and fearless, and in his wanderings we know that at least once he stayed with Father Marquette in Sault Ste. Marie.

Over the winter of 1672-1673 the two men made plans for their journey. They consulted what crude maps they had, laid in supplies, and recruited some Indian helpers. As spring approached, they were anxious to be off; but they delayed their start, knowing that the weather could be treacherous, and blizzards were not unknown in the latter part of April. In early May the last preparations were made, and on May 16 they left St. Ignace in two birch-bark canoes, with five assistants, supplies of corn and smoked meat, and the intention to live off the land as much as possible. They also took along a map they had projected from Indian reports. Each man agreed to keep his own journal and make his own maps. Marquette tells of the preparations: "Because we were going to seek strange countries, we took every precaution in our power, so that if our undertaking was hazardous, it should not be foolhardy. We obtained what information we could from the savages who had frequented those regions, and we traced out from their reports a map of the unknown lands. On it we indicated the rivers we were to navigate and the tribes we were to visit. Above all, I placed our expedition under the care of the Holy and Immaculate Virgin." He closes this section on preparations with the pledge: "We were ready to do and suffer everything for so glorious an undertaking."

The explorers traveled along the northern shore of Lake Michigan, paddling at the rate of four miles an hour. At night they made camp, and Father Marquette tells how they cooked wild rice, which he called "oats," for their evening meal. They entered Green Bay and made their way to its end where the Fox River began or, more properly, ended, since it emptied into the bay. They spent some time at a Mascouten (Potawatomi) Indian village and then they set out again on June 10, joined by two Miami Indians who would help them on the difficult portage between the Fox and Wisconsin Rivers. Finally the Wisconsin was reached, the Indian guides left, and Father Marquette recorded in his journal: "We left behind the waters that flowed toward Quebec and entered those that flowed toward the Mississippi."

For seven days they paddled down the Wisconsin and then on June 17, 1763, their canoes shot out of the Wisconsin into a mighty stream "a mile wide." They knew they had reached the Great River. Up to this point Father Marquette's diary had been episodic; but from here on, it became very detailed, as if he recognized the importance and newness of what he was recording. No item was too small to mention: from the variety of fish in the river to its gray geese, the drinking buffaloes, and even the shape of its banks. The size and speed of the buffaloes, which he called "wild cattle," amazed him. The travelers were particularly wary of Indians, since they didn't know whether the inhabitants of the areas they were passing through would be hostile or friendly.

They encountered their first Indians on June 25 — two villages of Illinois. They found the Indians friendly and hospitable. The Indians were amazed to discover a white man who knew their language. Before the travelers left, Father Marquette was presented with a sacred calumet, or peace pipe, made of red sandstone and decorated with feathers. The Illinois chief assured them that it would serve as a passport with other Indians, although he suggested that they turn back because there were many dangers ahead. Thanking the chief for his concern, the explorers went on, passing rivers that are now a litany of states — Iowa, Missouri, Illinois, Ohio, Arkansas. Several times they were threatened by bands of unfriendly Indians, but the calumet saved them. They passed empty riverbanks on which great American cities would be built, and the Frenchmen who followed the trail they blazed would leave behind such names as Prairie du Chien, Dubuque, Des Moines, St. Louis, Cape Girardeau.

The Marquette-Jolliet expedition's main difficulty now became one of language. The explorers had gone beyond the tribes with whom they could converse. The Indians became more hostile. Off the banks of one village a war club flew by Marquette's head. Before another village the expedition faced drawn bows. Each time Marquette's calumet saved the group. At last the explorers reached an Arkansas (Quapaw) Indian village where they tried one tongue after another until finally an old warrior was found who knew some Illinois. Through the interpreter they learned that the Indians ahead were allied with white men who were not of their speech. Thus they realized that they had reached the area of Spanish penetration. Knives, hatchets, and beads gave evidence of Spanish trading. That night some braves insisted that the seven white men be killed and their supplies seized. The chief would not consent and the next morning through the interpreter he told the French of the danger.

The travelers held a council. They knew now that the Great River emptied into the Gulf of Mexico. To go on risked arrest and imprisonment by the Spanish but more importantly the confiscation of their journals and maps. All the information they had gained for France would be lost and would be used by Spain. They had accomplished what Frontenac had charged them to do, and their findings would open the way for other explorers and traders. Moreover, it would be best to get back to one of the missions before winter arrived; they also knew the trip home would be more difficult, since they would have to paddle against the flow of the river. The conclusion of the meeting was that it was time to go home.

The decision, as it turned out, was a wise one. Father Marquette was not feeling well. He had contracted something on the trip down the Mississippi River, whether from food, water, or the bite of some bug, he knew not. But it became evident, as the travelers laboriously paddled against the current, that he was weakening. They decided to try a shortcut to Lake Michigan via the Illinois River and were happy to find an Illinois Indian village not long after they entered the river which would bear the tribe's name. They rested at the village three days, enjoying the hospitality of the ever-friendly Illinois. When they left, the chief sent some braves to help with the portages. It is not clear whether they portaged to the Calumet or Chicago River, but they did reach the southern end of Lake Michigan where their guides left them. With Marquette's strength visibly waning, the explorers finally reached St. Francis Xavier Mission. They had completed a journey of twenty-five hundred miles; but from the priest's diary it is difficult to judge what he considered more important — the discovery of a way to the Mississippi, or the baptism at the end of the expedition of a dying Indian child before it began its journey to heaven.

The two travelers spent the winter at St. Francis Xavier preparing their reports and maps: Jolliet for Frontenac and Marquette for his Jesuit superior. Marquette's health seemed to improve, and by the time the ice was out and the waters opened in the spring, he was more like his old self. Jolliet finally left for the long journey to Quebec, accompanied by his French boatmen and an Indian boy who was being sent by his chief to go to school. But tragedy lay ahead. Jolliet wrote Frontenac thus: "I was nearing home full of joy at the success of a long and difficult voyage. There seemed nothing more to fear, when a sudden gale capsized my canoe. I lost two men and my box of papers within sight of Montreal. Nothing remains to me but my life and the ardent desire to employ it in any service you may choose to direct." The two drowned boatmen were veterans of the Mississippi journey. Also drowned was the Indian boy. In Quebec, Jolliet wrote a second journal and drew new maps from memory; but when Marquette's records reached Quebec in the autumn of 1674, they became the official account and probably led to the crediting of the priest as the leader of the expedition.

Louis Jolliet was destined to embark on other missions for New France. The year following the Mississippi journey, he married the daughter of a wealthy trader. He went on explorations to Hudson Bay and Labrador. He was granted the islands of Mignan and Anticosti, where he established fisheries. Frontenac also appointed him royal pilot of the St. Lawrence. He died in 1700, aged fifty-five, and was buried on the island of Mignan, loyal to God and king.

Father Jacques Marquette was deemed healthy enough in the autumn of 1674 to start a new mission among his beloved Illinois. Why he and two French boatmen left in October for the village on the Illinois River is not clear. With winter coming on, it was an inauspicious time. Perhaps Marquette was overeager to get back to the Illinois Indians. In retrospect it was not a wise decision. The weather turned bad, and the journey down Lake Michigan was made in choppy waters against high winds. An early snowstorm delayed the travelers in a crude shelter. When they entered the Chicago River on December 4, ice blocked the way. On the site of present-day Chicago the boatmen built a log hut where the winter could be spent. Marquette was so ill that he could not say Mass on December 8, the feast of the Immaculate Conception of Our Lady. The three men subsisted there over the winter, with Marquette's health seesawing. On March 28 the ice broke with a roar and the travelers had to flee to high ground to escape the flood. It was mid-April when they reached the Illinois village.

Father Marquette realized that the plans he made for the conversion of the Illinois were not to be fulfilled by him. He was well enough to offer an outdoor Mass on Easter Sunday, but he knew his strength was ebbing. He told the Illinois that another Blackrobe would come among them. For himself he resolved to go back, to find a priest to whom he could confess and be near for the last rites of his Church. He wanted to get word to his superior to plead for a replacement for these most receptive Indians. On the journey back he could not paddle but instead lay prostrate and helpless on the bottom of the canoe. The travelers once again reached Lake Michigan and began the journey north. Marquette could not retain food. On May 18, 1675, the ailing priest knew he could go no farther. He asked the boatmen to put in to shore where there was a rise in the bank. A camp was made, and Marquette lay on a mat near the fire. He gave instructions for his burial and then told his companions to get some sleep, that he would call them if they were needed.

The boatmen slept for three hours when the call came. He asked one of the men to take the crucifix from

around his neck and hold it before his eyes. Murmuring "Jesus! Mary!" Father Marquette died. He was buried at the top of the bank, and a cross was made to serve as a marker for his grave. The two boatmen returned to St. Ignace at the upper end of the lake with the missioner's few possessions and his diary, this time ill-kept because of his sickness, and reported his death.

For two years the body of Jacques Marquette lay alone in the wilderness until a band of Indians hunting game found the cross marking their friend's grave. With a delicacy and tact not generally associated with Indians, they exhumed the body, cleansed and wrapped the bones, and set out to take them to St. Ignace. On June 8 the missioners at St. Ignace saw a procession of thirty canoes approaching. They received the remains of their confrere, said a requiem Mass for him, and then buried the bones beneath the chapel floor. In time the chapel burned down and Marquette's remains were forgotten. Then in 1877 a pastor at St. Ignace began excavating and found what was left. Some fragments were transported to Marquette University in Milwaukee where they are now enshrined. The remainder are at St. Ignace. But the best monument to the priest who found the way to the heart of America is in the country which lies to the south of his resting place.

# CHAPTER 3

## *The Missouri Traveler*

### *Pierre Jean De Smet*

In these days of superhighways and jet planes, travel is measured not so much in distance covered as the time spent en route. A five-mile trip on the Long Island Expressway at a time when traffic is at its peak might take an hour, while at a more favorable time of day it can be done in slightly more than five minutes. Hence it cannot always be appreciated that only a little more than a century ago the speed of travel was measured by the pace of a man or a horse or the breath of wind behind a sail.

With this in mind, it is truly remarkable that Father Pierre Jean De Smet covered the amazing total of some two hundred thousand miles in his missionary journeys in behalf of the American Indian. We know this figure because he kept a careful record of his daily activities and seemed to take some satisfaction in the distances he traveled. This was done at a time when railroads did not go west of the Mississippi and only a few river steamers plied the oftentimes treacherous Missouri.

Father De Smet was born in Termonde, Belgium, on January 30, 1801. His father, Joost De Smet, was a shipowner and his family was reasonably well off. As a boy he thought of becoming a soldier; but as he approached his teens, his ambition turned toward the priesthood and he entered the seminary at Mechelen. He was there when Father Charles Nerinckx came to give a talk to the students.

Father Nerinckx was in Europe to recruit priests and Sisters and raise funds for the Kentucky mission. De Smet and another seminarian told Father Nerinckx that they would like to return to America with him. The two boys left Europe without telling their parents because, as Father De Smet later pointed out, "To have asked consent of our parents, would have been to court a certain and absolute refusal."

Father Nerinckx paid for their trip to America and escorted his recruits to Baltimore where he entered them in Maryland's Jesuit novitiate. Not long afterward, the Jesuits decided to open a foundation in Western America — their first since their suppression — for the purpose of training missioners to the Indians. St. Louis was chosen, as it was the jumping-off place for those headed into the wilderness. When De Smet and his seven companions arrived there in 1823, St. Louis was a squalid town of four thousand people, a terminus for the fur trade, boasting one Catholic church. At the time of De Smet's death there in 1873, the town had become a city of some four hundred thousand, with thirty-six Catholic parishes.

Father De Smet was ordained to the priesthood on September 23, 1827, in Florissant, Missouri. He was a big-boned man, weighing over two hundred pounds, wearing his hair parted at the left side and keeping it long and over his ears in the fashion of the times. Although he was to survive cholera, smallpox, and black measle epidemics, he often suffered from ill health. Because of his gregarious nature and poor health, his superiors kept him in St. Louis doing promotional tasks. By 1833 his health was so poor that he was sent back to Europe to recuperate. He was taken ashore at Deal, England, to prevent his dying on the ship. When he was well enough he went to his family in Belgium, where he regained his strength. He was not to return to the United States until 1837.

The year following his return to St. Louis, De Smet was sent to open a mission among the Potawatomis near the site of modern-day Council Bluffs, Iowa. It was here that he came up against the reality of mission work among the Indians who were being demoralized by the American Fur Company which traded hard liquor for furs. It was an entrenched system, and De Smet did not gain popularity among the American traders in trying to fight it. It was here too that he learned that the Indian tribes were usually at war among themselves and here that he found his career as peacemaker. He journeyed north into Sioux lands to make a peace treaty between the Sioux and Potawatomis. It was here too that he had the encounter that was to influence his later life.

A band of Flathead Indians came to the American Fur Company to trade their fur harvest. When they learned that there was a mission among the Potawatomis, they came to De Smet and asked that a Blackrobe be sent among them to teach them about Jesus. They had heard about Christ and the Catholic Church from French voyageurs who had come among them seeking furs and from other Indians whom they had met at Hudson's Bay Company trading posts. They had gone to St. Louis years earlier seeking a priest, but that was before the Jesuits had settled there and no priest was available. De Smet was intrigued by their determination, but he was subject to obedience and could do nothing on his own. He sent them to St. Louis to see the bishop and also sent a letter saying he would be happy with such an assignment. The answer came back that he was to go among the Flatheads, survey the scene, and report back.

The Flathead territory was in what is now the north-west corner of Montana on the western side of the Continential Divide, of which the center was the Bitterroot Valley, now part of the Flathead Indian Reservation. It was a difficult five-month trek through plains, forests, and mountains to reach these people; but once there, Father De Smet's heart went out to them. Some of the Indians had learned the rudiments of Christianity and were practicing it as best they could. What especially pleased De Smet was that the tribe was well removed from the evils of white civilization. As part of his Jesuit training, he had studied the Paraguay reductions (resettlement communities), those tremendous experiments in Christian living that the Jesuits had introduced in South America, only to have the system collapse with the suppression of the Society of Jesus. De Smet pictured in his mind new reductions, this time in the Northwest. He promised the Indians that he would be back with helpers and supplies. The journey to the Flatheads took five months, and the return to St. Louis — this time via the Yellowstone and Missouri Rivers — would be about the same; but De Smet thought no more of the fatigue and difficulties than if it were an everyday affair. During this journey he came to know and be known by the tribes he would deal with over the years — Sioux, Crow, Blackfoot, Shoshone, Cheyenne, Omaha, and others.

True to his word, the following year (1841) he was on his way back. He was accompanied by two other priests, three lay brothers, a guide, and a number of wagons loaded with supplies. The first part of the trip was in the company of a wagon train headed for California. It was no easy journey over unmarked trails — west to Utah, north through Idaho into Montana. They had left in the spring and it was mid-August when they reached Fort Hall and the Hudson's Bay Company trading post, near what is now Pocatello, Idaho. Here they replenished their supplies of flour, sugar, and salt and were met by guides from the Flatheads who had been awaiting them. Then it was north to the Bitterroot Valley, where they established St. Mary's Mission, amid spectacular scenery: the Rocky Mountains to the east and the Bitterroot Mountains to the west.

Frequently during the journey, Father De Smet had spoken to his companions about his dream of establishing new reductions, building the kingdom of God on earth. It was a dream that he was never to realize fully because American troops and the white settlers behind them moved more rapidly than he could have guessed. He died thinking he had failed; but several years after his death, Senator George Vest — after a trip to investigate Indian conditions — rose up in Congress to declare: "I defy anyone to find me a single tribe of Indians on the plains — blanket Indians — that approximate the civilization of the Flatheads, who have been under the control of the Jesuits for fifty years. I say that out of the eleven tribes I saw — and I say this as a Protestant — where they had Protestant missionaries, they had not made a single solitary advance toward civilization: not one. Yet among the Flatheads, where there were two Jesuit missions [St. Mary's and St. Ignatius], you find farms, you find civilization, you find Christianity, you find the relation of husband and wife and of father and child scrupulously observed." Of course, much of this tribute belonged to Father De Smet's

31

companions and other Jesuits who came after them, but it was De Smet's vision that made the missions among the Flatheads unique.

St. Mary's Mission provided a good base for Father De Smet to visit other tribes. In 1842 he traveled to Fort Colville (in the northeast corner of what is now Washington state) and Fort Vancouver (near present-day Portland, Oregon). He was able to contact such tribes as the Pend d'Oreille (Kalispel), Nez Percé, Kutenai, and Blackfoot. He preached the Gospel and he baptized those who were ready. He was the first priest most of these Indians saw, and his baptisms were counted in the thousands. He became an authority on the Indian nations. He faithfully recorded his journeyings and his observations, and his journals are a prime research source. He learned the geography and trails of the West and knew as much as any scout or mountain man. His highways were rivers like the Columbia, Yellowstone, and Missouri.

Yet mission work cannot succeed without funds, personnel, and supplies — and these were always needed. He returned to St. Louis to plead for more aid; but the Jesuits had little to give, and it was recommended that he go begging. He went to New Orleans and Boston, making appeals for aid. He was successful in raising money, but personnel were scarce in a burgeoning America that needed all its priests and Sisters for the waves of immigrants that were arriving. Recalling how he himself was recruited, De Smet decided to go to Europe. He visited Ireland, England, France, Belgium, Italy, and Holland. While on this trip he learned that he was being considered as a candidate for bishop of Oregon. He did everything he could to avert this, and during a visit to Rome even told the Holy Father that he was not the man for the job. He promoted for the post Father Francis N. Blanchet who was representing the archbishop of Quebec in the area, and it was Blanchet who was finally chosen and became the founder of the Church in the Northwest.

The begging journey was so successful that Father De Smet was able to charter the brig *Indefatigable* to transport his supplies and personnel. With a ship of his own, at least temporarily, he decided to go around Cape Horn and across the Pacific to Astoria in Oregon. It would save the long trip across the breadth of the United States and get him back to the Bitterroot Valley sooner. It would also be easier for his recruits, particularly the six Sisters of Notre Dame de Namur he had signed up for the Indian missions. He worried about the Italian priests who had joined him because he knew the climate that awaited them, a climate far different from their sunny Italy. Even so, the trip was not an easy one. Stops were made in Chile and Peru for supplies and repairs. Finally, Astoria, Oregon, was reached.

With the new personnel and supplies he had brought back with him, De Smet was able to start two new missions — St. Francis Xavier (on the Willamette River) and St. Ignatius (north of St. Mary's, near Flathead Lake). He spent the winter at this latter mission among the Kalispel Indians. Then, although the season was late, he journeyed into the Blackfoot country of British Columbia and Alberta. He arrived at Fort Edmonton on December 31. He hired a dogsled and went north to the Atabasca River. When the ice went out, he returned to St. Mary's by way of the Columbia River.

From 1846 on, the nature of Father De Smet's work

changed. He had now become a roving ambassador, forming friendships with the various tribes and pleading their cause before the American government. That same year he concluded a peace treaty between the Blackfeet and the Flatheads. He journeyed into the Sioux country, exploring the Badlands. He was said to have discovered gold there but kept silent because he did not wish an army of white gold seekers to disturb Indian life. In 1849 he followed the Santa Fe Trail, visiting Osage, Shawnee, Miami, and other Indian tribes. In 1851 the government asked him to attend the great peace council at Fort Laramie in Wyoming. He used the occasion to baptize nearly sixteen hundred Indians. At the request of the secretary of war, he accepted in 1858 a commission as chaplain in the U.S. Army in order to accompany General William S. Harney on his expedition to put down the Mormon rebellion known as the Utah War. They never reached Utah because word came while they were at South Platte that the rebellion was over. The party returned to St. Louis where Harney received new orders to go to Oregon where the Flatheads and Coeur d'Alenes had risen to resist the incursions of white settlers.

Father De Smet had little respect for General Harney, since the latter had a reputation as an Indian killer. To end the Seminole War, he had executed thirteen chiefs by hanging them. In the battle of Ash Hollow he had not spared women and children. However, De Smet agreed to go to Oregon with the American officer in the hope that he could parlay vengeance into justice. The party went to New York and sailed to Panama, where a railroad had been built across the isthmus to accommodate the California gold seekers. On the Pacific side they took passage on a ship to Oregon, reaching Fort Vancouver in October, only to learn that the Indian rebellion had been quelled and peace made with the aid of the Jesuit missioners. Several troublemakers had been hanged, and each tribe had delivered a chief and four families as hostages.

De Smet defended the Indians before General Harney, explaining their point of view as whites moved into their lands. In the end General Harney ordered the priest to visit the tribes near Fort Vancouver to bind up their wounds and urge them to keep the peace. De Smet then used his powers of persuasion to get the general to agree to release the Coeur d'Alene hostages into his custody and return them to their people. Surprisingly, the general agreed. The priest spent the winter with the Coeur d'Alenes and in the spring went to the Kalispels, Flatheads, and other tribes. He returned to Fort Vancouver and made his report, then he went back overland to St. Louis via Fort Benton — no easy trip for an aging man whose health was far from good. He continued to represent Indian interests in the following years both in Washington and on the frontier. When there was a peace mission to be made, he was the first one the government considered.

Father De Smet's most spectacular peace mission took place in 1868 and it was to the Sioux along the Powder River. He had cemented a previous peace between the government and the Sioux which had only lasted until gold was discovered and hordes of prospectors invaded Sioux land. The Sioux began killing whites indiscriminately, giving no quarter and asking none. Because of many broken promises, Chief Sitting Bull and other Sioux leaders understandably refused to meet with government officials. De Smet was asked to contact the Sioux and to convince them to undertake peace talks. Although he had little hope of any lasting success, he knew that any truce meant the saving of lives on both sides. It was not a challenge without risk, since the Sioux were killing all white men they ran across. The Blackrobe not only had to locate Sitting Bull but to get into and out of his camp alive.

Father De Smet traveled up the Missouri River on the steamer of his good friend Captain Joseph LaBarge to Fort Rice, where he found a beehive of activity as the soldiers prepared for war. A trader at the fort was an old friend by the name of Charles E. Galpin, an Iowan who had married Eagle Woman, the daughter of a Teton-Sioux chief. Eagle Woman was to be De Smet's passport to the hostiles. Friendly Sioux chiefs who were at Fort Rice for protection refused to send any of their braves with the priest because of the certainty of death they believed awaited. De Smet told them that God's angels would protect them, that back in St. Louis children were praying for him. "If the angels are going with you, we will go also," one of the chiefs told him. Eagle Woman said that she too would go.

When the party left Fort Rice for the Powder River, where it was believed Sitting Bull was camped, it consisted of two wagons full of presents, seventy braves, ten squaws, and Major Galpin and his wife. Major Galpin did not have the confidence in the angels that Father De Smet and the Indians had, and he worried about what lay ahead. It was the usual hard journey during which De Smet frequently vomited blood and suffered from swollen ankles which made walking difficult and painful for him. They sent out scouts, and finally contact was made with Sitting Bull. One day a party of Sitting Bull's warriors came to the camp. They said that Sitting Bull would receive De Smet but no other white man. Eagle Woman reported that one of the braves who was indebted to her family had told her that Sitting Bull intended to kill the Blackrobe and the friendly Sioux when they entered his camp. Undaunted, De Smet said he would go forward and the others said they would go with him. They pushed on, and some days later they were suddenly surrounded by Sioux in war paint. De Smet raised his banner of the Blessed Virgin and told his companions to offer no resistance. The hostiles surrounded the group and led it forward to an Indian camp. De Smet, Galpin, and Galpin's wife were put into one tepee where the priest immediately fell asleep as if he were back in the safety of St. Louis.

The next morning the Jesuit was taken to meet Sitting Bull. Father De Smet told the chief he had dared to come and see him because he knew that Sitting Bull's heart was good, since the Indian leader loved his people so much that he was willing to die for them. Sitting Bull replied that the whites had provoked the war and that as a result he had done all the hurt to the whites that he could and that he would not sign white men's papers because those who did so were now starving. For a long time Sitting Bull listed Indian complaints. The Blackrobe replied that he had no power to correct wrongs, but nothing could be done unless Sitting Bull made his complaints directly to the army. The Indian chief replied that he did not trust the white men and if he was killed there would be no one to lead the Sioux. Back and forth the arguments went until finally it was decided to send another chief in Sitting

Bull's place, a great warrior named Gall who had proved himself fearless against the whites. De Smet replied that he would stand guarantee for Gall's life.

Thus the peace commission met at Fort Rice. Gall led a delegation of Sioux — among them Yankton, Brulé, and Miniconjou. He stated the complaints of the Indians. The peace commission pledged to remove the forts from the Powder River country, and Gall signed a peace treaty in the name of Sitting Bull. Once again Father De Smet had succeeded when all other government efforts had failed. Unfortunately, like other treaties, it would be broken by uncaring whites which would lead to the Big Horn massacre and the enshrinement of Sitting Bull in the pages of American history. The Powder River concessions were De Smet's last big hurrah. There would be another trip to Europe to raise aid for the missions and another trek into the Badlands to establish a Sioux mission, but old age and ill health ended his prairie life. Now his days were spent at his desk in St. Louis writing the history of the Missouri Jesuit province. His once large body, inclined to fat, was now painfully thin; his once sturdy legs now had difficulty supporting him. One day his friend Captain LaBarge came to call. The riverman had just built a new boat, three hundred sixty-three feet long, boasting thick carpets and cut-glass chandeliers in its common rooms. He told the priest that there would always be a cabin for him and now a large place to say Mass. De Smet had heard of the boat but was unaware of Captain LaBarge's surprise. It was to be named the *De Smet*. Was Father strong enough to bless the boat on Friday? Father De Smet promised that he would be there. Although Friday was a drizzly, cold day, the old missioner preserved his reputation for keeping a promise. When he returned from the blessing, he took to his bed and died there at two o'clock on the morning of May 23, 1873. He was buried in the Jesuit cemetery at Florissant.

# *PART*
# *TWO*

## The Pioneers □ *INTRODUCTION*

If a pioneer is one who leads the way into uncharted areas, there were many pioneers in American Catholicism. Not only were there those who moved west with the expanding American frontier, but there were pioneers in education, charity, the press, ecumenism, and sundry other interests. In the broad sense, all of the people in this book were pioneers. But for the purpose of clarity, the use of the word here is limited to those who brought the Church to pagan lands and whose work laid the foundation for missions, parishes, and dioceses yet to come. Even with this limitation, there were many.

There were priests like Father Demetrius Augustine Gallitzin, the Russian convert-prince, who brought Catholicism to the wilderness of Pennsylvania; Gabriel Richard, a genius of a man who represented Michigan in Congress and helped lay the foundation for the University of Michigan; the Franciscan Antonio Margil, who built a series of missions across Texas; in the Southwest, extraordinary characters, such as the inventive Eusebio Kino and the patient Archbishop John Lamy.

To represent these trailblazers of Catholic civilization

and culture, three have been chosen: one for the East and one for the West (who were contemporaries but unaware of each other's existence), and one whose mission was the world.

# CHAPTER 4

## The First Family
### The Carrolls

It is not unusual to come across the mistaken notion that the American Revolution patriots Charles Carroll, Daniel Carroll, and John Carroll were brothers or that they belonged to the same Carroll family. In fact, Daniel and John were siblings and Charles a second cousin. The relationship came not through any Carroll ancestors — those tracers of lineage have never been able to find a common Carroll ancestor — but through the Darnall family. Charles Carroll's grandmother was a Darnall, as was the mother of Daniel and John. The common ancestor was Colonel Henry Darnall (1645-1711), whose daughter Mary married Charles Carroll the Settler — the pair becoming grandparents to Charles Carroll of Carrollton. Eleanor Darnall (Colonel Darnall's granddaughter) married Daniel Carroll of Upper Marlboro, and the two were the parents of Daniel Carroll of Rock Creek and John Carroll the bishop. To complicate matters even further, Charles Carroll of Carrollton married Mary Darnall, his own cousin and that of Daniel and John. The intermingling of the Carroll and Darnall families came about because they were the wealthiest and most prominent Catholic families in Maryland in particular and in all the British colonies in general, going back to the very foundation of the Maryland colony.

Maryland had its origin in the Stuart restoration in

England. When George Calvert, the first Lord Baltimore, became a Catholic in 1625, he dreamed of a colony in the New World where Catholics would be free to practice their religion. He made application for such a grant but died before receiving it. Charles I gave George Calvert's son Cecil, the second Lord Baltimore, a charter naming him the first Lord Proprietor of the Maryland colony, a name derived not from the Virgin Mary — as many erroneously believe — but in honor of England's Queen Henrietta Maria, wife of Charles I. Cecil, a devout Catholic, was also practical. He realized that if the colony was to be successful, it needed a broader base; so in his articles of organization he decreed that full religious toleration would exist in the new colony and Christians of any faith would be welcome. Although this seemed to close the colony to Jews, it was not the case. For instance, a Jew named Jacob Lumbrozo settled there and, although he had some difficulties in 1658, lived peacefully and prosperously thereafter.

The Maryland colonists sailed from England on November 22, 1633, aboard the *Ark* and the *Dove*. Among the travelers were sixteen Catholic gentlemen and their families under the Catholic leadership of Leonard Calvert, brother of Cecil. (Leonard became the first governor of the colony.) There were many indentured servants, mostly Protestant. The ships made a detour to pick up four Jesuits — two priests (Andrew White and John Altham) and two Brothers. The first landing was made on an island in Chesapeake Bay and there on March 24, 1634, Father White offered the first Mass. The idyll started out well and in 1649 the Maryland colony passed the Act Concerning Religion (also called the Toleration Act), which again affirmed total freedom of worship. However, as Father John Tracy Ellis points out, bigotry was imported from the Virginia colony at Jamestown and found fertile ground among the Protestant majority in Maryland. From 1655 on, limitations began to be put upon Catholics who were denied the right to vote or hold office or erect churches. In 1704 a law was passed forbidding "Popish priests" from baptizing and, later, in 1756, Catholics were subjected to double taxation.

The Carroll ancestors did not come with the original colonists. Colonel Henry Darnall, brother-in-law of Lord Baltimore, arrived in Maryland in 1672, began large plantations, and before long was very wealthy. Charles Carroll the Settler arrived in Maryland in 1688. Although he became prosperous, his wealth was no match for that of Darnall. It was his son, Charles Carroll of Annapolis, who acquired great wealth which he passed on to his son, Charles Carroll of Carrollton, who in turn made it grow even larger. At the time of the American Revolution both branches of the Carroll families were among the richest families in the Thirteen Colonies.

## • CHARLES CARROLL, THE SIGNER

Charles Carroll of Carrollton was born on September 19, 1737, and took his early education at Bohemia Manor in Maryland where the Jesuit Fathers had set up a small school for Catholic children. It housed twenty boarders and an equal number of day students. When Charles was eleven, he was sent to a school run by exiled English Jesuits at St. Omer, in French Flanders. He was to be in

Europe sixteen years, studying in Rheims, Paris, and London. Well educated, he arrived back in Maryland early in 1765, when his father presented him with a ten-thousand-acre estate in Frederick County, named Carrollton, a title he added to his name for identification. He married an impoverished cousin, Mary Darnall, and set about enlarging the wealth his father had bestowed upon him.

Although his Catholic religion barred him from holding public office in Maryland, Charles Carroll developed an interest in the politics of his times. His opinion and support were sought by such leaders as William Paca and Samuel Chase. When the First Continental Congress met in Philadelphia in 1774, the Maryland colonists (who could not send him as a delegate) asked him to go as an observer because of the value of his opinion. In 1776 — along with Benjamin Franklin, Samuel Chase, and his cousin Bishop John Carroll — he was sent on a mission to Canada to seek help or at least a promise of neutrality. That same year he was instrumental in bringing Maryland into the independence movement and, with restrictive laws removed, was made a delegate to the Continental Congress and a member of the War Board.

On August 2 of that year, along with forty-eight other delegates, Charles signed the Declaration of Independence. (The remaining six affixed their signatures later on.) Also that same year he drafted the Maryland Constitution and promoted its acceptance by the Maryland Assembly. He was elected a delegate to the Federal Constitutional Convention in 1787 but declined, preferring to allow his cousin Daniel to represent the family. He did support the new Constitution, helping its ratification in Maryland. He was elected as Maryland's first senator to the United States Congress; but when a law was passed prohibiting one from serving both in the federal senate and state senate, he resigned the federal post to continue serving his state. In 1800 he founded the First Bank of the United States and in 1816 became one of the founding stockholders of the Second Bank of the United States. When on July 4, 1826, both Thomas Jefferson and John Adams died, Charles Carroll became the last surviving signer of the Declaration of Independence. In 1828, as a member of the board of directors, he laid the cornerstone for the Baltimore and Ohio Railroad. That year he became the president of the American Colonization Society. Charles Carroll died on November 14, 1832, at the age of ninety-five, in Baltimore. At his death he was one of the most prominent Catholic laymen in the United States. His funeral services were held in the Baltimore cathedral, and after the funeral rites a large cortege escorted his remains back to his estate where he was buried.

Shortly before his death, Charles Carroll wrote: "I have come almost to the threshold of ninety-six years; I have always enjoyed the best of health. I have been blessed with great riches, prosperity, public esteem, and more of the good things than the world usually concedes; but in looking back, the one thing that gives me the greatest satisfaction is that I practiced the duties of my religion."


## • DANIEL CARROLL, THE CONSTITUTIONALIST

Another Carroll who gained national prominence was Daniel Carroll of Rock Creek, brother of Bishop John

Carroll and cousin of Charles. Daniel was five years older than his brother, John, having been born in 1730. His father, Daniel Carroll of Upper Marlboro, had gained considerable wealth from his farms and a thriving mercantile business. His mother was Eleanor Darnall, and it was through her that he was related to the other Carroll branch of the family. When he was twelve he left Maryland for St. Omer in French Flanders to study under refugee English Jesuits. His studies there of St. Thomas Aquinas and St. Robert Bellarmine were to stand him in good stead for his later work on the American Constitution. He remained abroad for six years, returning in 1748 when he was eighteen to enter his father's businesses. Not long after, on reaching his majority, he was forced to become head of the family when his father died.

Daniel Carroll, Sr., had come to Maryland from Ireland sometime around 1720, settling on the Patuxent River where he opened a general store and acted as a trade middleman. Importing goods from England and exporting tobacco, he prospered and began buying lands on which to grow tobacco and other crops. His first purchase of land was recorded in 1725 and the following year he bought another five hundred acres in Howard County. In 1727 he courted and won the hand of Eleanor Darnall, who had also been educated abroad in France. She brought to the marriage two tracts of land which were her inheritance. When Daniel Carroll of Upper Marlboro died in 1751, he was a man rich in land, livestock, and slaves and had a prosperous import-export business.

Hardly out of his youth, Daniel Carroll II (who would be known as Daniel Carroll of Rock Creek) had to take over this business and be responsible for his mother, brother, and four sisters. He not only did this successfully but added to the family's wealth. In 1752 he married Eleanor Carroll, a distant cousin, by whom he had two children, both of whom he would outlive. His wife died in 1763 and it left him distraught. To regain his equilibrium, he journeyed to Europe, where he visited his brother, John, then studying on the Continent, and called on business connections in London.

When Daniel Carroll returned to the future United States, he again took up his business duties but also became involved — in 1777 — in Maryland political affairs and the growing independence movement. He served in the Continental Congress (1780-1784) and the House of Representatives (1780-1791). He also became a leader in the Maryland Senate (1777-1780). Thus he was a natural choice as a Maryland delegate to the Constitutional Convention in Philadelphia (1787-1788) where he had great influence. He was the leader in the fight against having the president elected by Congress. He wrote the Tenth Amendment to the Constitution which protected states' rights and played an important role in formulating the amendment which prohibited Congress from establishing any religion. In this latter effort he had, of course, his own religious experience in mind, and his intention was not that Congress should ignore religion but that another Church of England should not be established as a national church with preferential treatment.

When the Constitution was completed, Daniel returned to Maryland, where with his cousin Charles he led the debate for its acceptance. There was much opposition to various parts of the document, but he carried the day. In 1791 President George Washington appointed Daniel

Carroll to a three-man commission to select the site for the new national capital. Daniel was sorely tried in working with the temperamental Pierre L'Enfant, who had been selected as the architect for the project. Carroll lands were involved in L'Enfant's planning and on one occasion the Frenchman razed the house of Daniel's father-in-law because L'Enfant wanted the site for a fountain. Daniel Carroll transferred his own property — the portion that L'Enfant wanted — to the federal government. He personally picked the site for the Capitol, and today the Supreme Court Building stands on what was Carroll land. When in 1793 a cornerstone for Federal City (as it was then called) was laid, Daniel Carroll stood alongside President Washington for a Masonic ceremony of dedication.

Daniel Carroll was no stranger to Masonic ceremonies. While remaining a Catholic, he had joined the Masons in 1780. The president of the United States and many other national leaders were Masons. Daniel's brother, the bishop, did not approve of the association. When asked for his opinion, Bishop Carroll stated in writing: "Severe and heavy censures, even that of excommunication, have been denounced [announced publicly] by two successive Popes against all persons who continue in or join the Society and frequent the Lodges of Free Masons, and the reason alleged is that their meetings are found by experience to be destructive of morality and to diminish very much the habit of religious exercises. I do not pretend that these decrees are received generally by the Church, or have full authority in this diocese. But they ought to be a very serious warning to all good Christians not to expose themselves to dangers which the Supreme Head of the Church has judged to be contagious." Thus, while Daniel Carroll was within the law, the bishop let it be known that he would have preferred greater circumspection.

What the bishop did not know was that Daniel Carroll's attendance at ceremonies would be limited. In February 1796 Daniel's mother, Eleanor, died at the age of ninety-two. She had been active to the very end, running her Rock Creek estate which had increased in value under her care, her manor house alone employing twenty-four slaves. Daniel Carroll, whose wife had died many years earlier, had come to depend greatly on his mother, and her death was a great shock to him. Within three months of his mother's death, Daniel was himself dead. The *Gazette and Baltimore Daily Advertiser* reported: "Last May 7, died at Rock Creek, Daniel Carroll, Esq., a gentleman of unbounded philanthropy, and possessed of all the esteem of all who had the pleasure of his acquaintance."

With Daniel Carroll's death, both Maryland and the nation had lost a valued citizen. He had served both well. In his will Daniel had left his brother, the bishop (who was now the head of the family), "two acres of land comprehending and contiguous to the Roman Catholic Church." It was his gift to the bishop of St. John's Chapel on the family estate, the church where John Carroll in 1774 had picked up his priestly ministry in what was to be the United States.

## • JOHN CARROLL, THE FIRST BISHOP

If we were to draw up the qualifications of the man who was to found the Catholic hierarchy of the United States, we could not make a better description than that brought to the task by John Carroll. Not only was he a native of the future United States, but he also came from one of the wealthiest and oldest Catholic families in the country.

John Carroll was born on the manor of his parents, Daniel and Eleanor Darnall Carroll, in Upper Marlboro, Maryland, on January 8, 1735. His father, as already described, was a wealthy man through his own initiative; his mother was a cultured woman who had been educated in France. He was born during a time when Anglicans controlled what had been founded as a Catholic colony, and not only were Catholics proscribed from voting and holding public office but were subject to the most anti-Catholic laws of any of the colonies. As a result, Catholics were more determined than ever to preserve the faith of their children by teaching youngsters in their homes or in small schools supported by Catholic parents of the area. There was such a school at Bohemia Manor, one of the first permanent Catholic settlements, and it was there that John Carroll received his first formal education under the guidance of the Jesuit pastor Father Thomas Poulton.

In 1748 John's brother, Daniel (who was five years older), returned from Europe where he had gone to study, and it was decided to send John to take his place. It was about this time that the Maryland *Gazette* reported "great numbers of their Catholic youth were sent this year to foreign Popish seminaries." It was a great sacrifice for parents to send their children abroad, not only for the expense of transatlantic travel and foreign education but also because of the long separation that was necessary. The most popular foreign school of the time was St. Omer in French Flanders, which was conducted by exiled English Jesuits. It was recommended for "the Great Care taken of Youth, and the Cheapness of the Commons and Education there." Many of John's relatives had gone to St. Omer and it was to be expected that he would follow his brother.

Thus, at the end of the summer of 1748, John Carroll — going on fourteen — sailed from Annapolis, accompanied by his cousin Charles Carroll, two years younger, who was destined to sign America's Declaration of Independence, and another Bohemia classmate, Robert Brent. In Flanders the young Maryland aristocrats found a life much different from the ease they had known. St. Omer had been founded in 1592 to train Catholic English boys who were denied Catholic education in their homeland. It was strictly run and without frills. Charles Carroll was to observe later that its "education is only fit for priests," and he was to go on to other schools in France and England that would better prepare him for a business career. He did appreciate what his years at St. Omer did for him and was to comment many times on "the good practices I learned under the Jesuits."

While John Carroll was at St. Omer, his father died (1751), leaving his considerable estate to his two sons "to be equally divided between them as they shall severally arrive at the age of twenty-one." The will also enjoined Mrs. Carroll to continue John's education. Thus there was no question of John's going home and he probably would have objected to a recall. His sights were no longer on Maryland but on the Jesuits to whom he felt called. So in 1753 John Carroll went "up the hill" and entered the Jesuit novitiate, later passing on to the scholasticate in Liège. Because of the confusion of the times — the Jesuits were being attacked by France, Spain, and Portugal — it is not clear when John Carroll was ordained or when he made his final profession as a Jesuit. He may have already been a priest when his brother, Daniel, visited him in 1763; but more than likely he was not ordained until 1769. That visit may have been also the occasion when he renounced his inheritance in favor of his siblings. At any rate, he was ordained a Jesuit priest, spent some time visiting Jesuit establishments in Europe, and was then assigned to teaching at Liège and Bruges in Belgium.

John Carroll was in Bruges when the blow fell. The Jesuits were suppressed and on the night of October 14, 1773, police broke into the college at Bruges, arresting Father Carroll and other Jesuits. Father Carroll was released through the efforts of Lord Arundell of England. The other Jesuits decided to go to Liège and join a secularized college there. Father Carroll went to England with Lord Arundell, who offered him the post of family chaplain. Deeply upset by the destruction of the Society of Jesus, whose spirit so fitted his needs, Father Carroll had no desire to spend his remaining years as a private chaplain. He was forty years old, a difficult age to try and start anew; but if he was going to make a fresh start, he reasoned, the place to do it was in America — among friends and family and "removed from the scenes of distress of many of my dearest friends, whom God knows I shall not be able to relieve."

Father Carroll arrived back from Europe in mid-1774 to find a Maryland far different from what he remembered. Daniel welcomed him home and his sisters invited him to their estates. He chose to go to Rock Creek and live with his mother — there was a good-sized chapel there and

Catholics in the countryside whom he could serve. But the conversations around him made him aware that great change was in the air. The merchants complained of the taxation and limitations placed upon them by England, of how the mother country was keeping them from developing their own industry. Fiery slogans from Massachusetts made their way southward, and there was talk of rebellion against and separation from England. Maryland had even had its own destruction of tea. Furthermore, delegates from the colonies were meeting in Philadelphia to plan the results of freedom. It was this latter group that involved Father Carroll.

The Continental Congress had come to the conclusion that a break with England had to take place. It knew that the mother country would resist. What concerned many delegates was what position Canada would take. Most of the colonies had little use for Canada because it was mainly Catholic, and the Quebec Act — which had been bitterly denounced in the colonies — recognized and made privileged the Catholic religion there. Nevertheless, as independence was planned, politics became more important than prejudices. It was proposed that a committee be sent to Quebec. It would be the work of this committee to gain the support of the Canadians. Three men were appointed: Benjamin Franklin, Samuel Chase, and Charles Carroll (the latter because of his abilities, but more so because he was a Catholic). Yet even that committee could be improved. As Charles Lee of New York said: "I should think that if some Jesuit or Religieuse of any other Order (but he must be a man of liberal sentiments, enlarged mind and a manifest friend to Civil Liberty) could be found out and sent to Canada, he would be worth battalions to us. . . . Mr. Carroll has a relative who exactly answers the description."

The relative was, of course, Father John Carroll — and he was added to the group. Father Carroll was not sanguine about what the committee could accomplish. Canada's grievances had been settled in the Quebec Act and Catholics there were quite happy with their lot. The French clergy were also well aware of the bigotry that existed in New England, particularly in Massachusetts. Moreover, Father Carroll must have had the suspicion that he was being used, yet he had identified with the patriot cause and could not refuse. The journey north by the ambassadors was a difficult one and the Canadian reception was cool. Father Carroll argued that the Continental Congress had promised to respect the individual conscience and give free exercise of religion once independence was obtained, but the Canadians informed him they already had these things. The Canadians had long memories and cited a number of bigoted acts south of their border. The other ambassadors were also unproductive. The Canadians believed the independence movement was certain to fail because the Americans lacked money, credit, and supplies. There was no meeting of minds. Benjamin Franklin was the first to give up and Father Carroll agreed to return home with him. The others soon followed. The Canadian venture turned out to be a failure.

Back at his parish of St. John, Father Carroll had his own juridical status to worry about. With the Jesuits dissolved he had no religious superior or affiliation. The colonies had been under the jurisdiction of the bishop of London; but with the war in progress, his delegate in the colonies — Father John Lewis — was in limbo. Besides, there was the matter of Jesuit properties in the United States: they had to be protected and administered. There were also the matters of discipline and assignment of clergy, and means for their regular support. The Carrolls had a reputation for organization, and Father Carroll put that skill to work. In June of 1783 he called a meeting of priests to be held at Whitemarsh, the former Jesuit residence on the Annapolis Road. The meeting resulted in establishing a "Select Body of Clergy." The group sent a message to the Congregation of Propaganda in Rome (now called the Sacred Congregation for the Evangelization of Peoples and the Propagation of the Faith), asking that Father Lewis be appointed superior with the power to bless chalices, holy oils, and altar stones, and be authorized to administer confirmation. Someone had to be in charge.

The Holy See decided to solve the American matter with the help of France, recognizing that the French alliance with and aid to the colonies gave it influence with the new American government. The papal nuncio to France consulted with Benjamin Franklin, the American envoy to France. Franklin, surprised, let it be known that having just freed themselves from foreign domination, American Catholics would prefer one of their own as leader. He also spoke highly of his friend Father Carroll, recalling the priest's many kindnesses when he had returned home ill from Canada. At the same time he told the surprised nuncio that the United States government could not interfere in the affairs of a church. Rome weighed the matter and decided to move slowly. In 1784 Father Carroll was named "Superior of the Mission in the provinces of the new Republic of the United States of North America."

Father Carroll turned his attention to the school he

wanted to establish. He desired an institution of such quality that young men would no longer have to travel to Europe to find suitable Catholic education. It was not an easy task, for money had to be raised, tutors hired, courses set, a location chosen, and buildings erected. A headmaster was found in Robert Plunkett, a priest who had come to the Maryland mission from the English College at Douay. Two Catholic gentlemen donated land on the "Potowmack River." A committee of prominent people — Charles Carroll of Carrollton, John Darnall of Maryland, Thomas FitzSimons of Philadelphia, Dominick Lynch of New York, among others — was set up to raise funds. He met a bit of opposition from some clergy, particularly ex-Jesuits; but he moved ahead, assuring the former Jesuits that should the society be reestablished in his lifetime, the Georgetown College would be turned over to it.

Meanwhile, it became apparent that the problem of jurisdiction of the new superior general was of necessity only a stopgap measure. The superior's powers were limited, and the ordination of new priests would have to take place in Canada or Europe. Father Carroll suggested to Rome that the American clergy nominate one of their own as bishop. Rome agreed, and an election was held at Whitemarsh which Carroll won. His name was forwarded to Propaganda. Again Rome consulted through Paris, and Thomas Jefferson (then in Paris as envoy) replied that Father Carroll's appointment would not give offense to either "our institutions or opinions." Rome simply did not understand the American concept of freedom of religion and its separation of Church and State.

On September 14, 1789, Pope Pius VI approved the choice of John Carroll, and America had its first bishop.

Since he could not be consecrated in the United States and he recalled his cold reception in Canada, Father Carroll chose to go to England. A friendship made when he was stationed in Europe now proved its worth. Thomas Weld, owner of Lulworth Castle, had built there England's first Catholic church since the Reformation. It would be a privilege to have Father Carroll consecrated in it. Thus, on the feast of the Assumption in 1790, Father Carroll received the fullness of orders. A witness recorded that Thomas Weld "omitted no circumstances which could possibly add dignity to so venerable a ceremony."

Bishop Carroll was back in the United States in early December. Rome had named Baltimore as the see city for the new diocese. The Baltimore *Advertiser* reported on December 10, "On Tuesday last the ship Samson, Capt. Thomas Moore, arrived from London. In this vessel came as a passenger the Rt. Rev. Dr. John Carroll, recently consecrated Bishop of the Catholic Church in the United States. On the landing of this learned and worthy prelate he was respectfully waited on by a number of his fellow citizens of various denominations who conducted him to his residence."

There was one immediate project that Bishop Carroll wanted to launch. The American Church had many problems, the result of wide separation of parishes and some disorganization. He was also worried lest a spirit would develop among the clergy that would separate them from Rome. He wanted his clergy to be American but under the spiritual guidance of the pope. To meet these problems, he decided to call a synod.

The first synod to be held in the United States opened in Baltimore on November 7, 1791, with twenty priests present. The synod adopted rules for baptism, confirmation, and the Eucharist. Support of the local church and pastor was to come from Sunday collections, one third of which was to be reserved for the poor. Children were to be admitted to first Holy Communion at the age of reason but only after full instruction in Catholic doctrine and a general confession. Only confessions made to priests with proper faculties were valid. Rules were drawn up for mixed marriages. The synod thus gave a direction to the Church which would affect future generations.

While in Europe for his consecration, Bishop Carroll had been in contact with Sulpician Fathers. One of them, Father Charles Nagot, had gone to London on the instructions of his superior general to discuss the possibility of work in America. Bishop Carroll immediately saw the advantage of having these trained educators. Although he was not sure the time was ripe for an American seminary, he believed they could help in educating American Catholics. He invited them to Baltimore. It was an act for which he was criticized. Georgetown saw a rival in the Sulpicians, some of the ex-Jesuits were unhappy at another society taking root, and there was an anti-Gallic spirit on the part of others. But history has proven that in bringing the Sulpicians to the United States, Bishop Carroll made one of the wisest moves of his episcopate.

The Sulpicians arrived the year following Carroll's consecration. The Sulpician superior did not send second-raters but priests with reputations as theologians and philosophers. They also brought with them five seminarians from England, Canada, and France, and a young American convert; so the matter of establishing a seminary was academic. They rented One-Mile Tavern, just outside the city limits, and this three-story red brick building became the first St. Mary's Seminary. In 1799 the Sulpicians began St. Mary's Academy, a competition with Georgetown which Bishop Carroll did not prevent. Within a decade the seminary had enrolled half a hundred candidates for the priesthood, of whom twenty-eight were eventually ordained. St. Mary's truly became the cradle of the American Catholic Church. Father John Dubois shortly afterward founded Mount St. Mary's at Emmitsburg, and between the two institutions came a stream of priests who were to become bishops and leaders in spreading Catholicism.

The year 1796 was a difficult one for Bishop Carroll. Early in the year, his mother, to whom he had always stayed close, died at the age of ninety-two. The bishop and his brother, Daniel, were appointed executors of her estate. Three months later, Daniel died suddenly. John had become the head of his branch of the Carroll family and would have to carry its temporal responsibilities. Three years later the pope died. Carroll had been in contact with Pope Pius VI in the hope of getting a coadjutor in case of his own death. In December of 1799 George Washington passed away, about four months after the death of Pius VI. The former president had been a good friend to Carroll. When the bishop suggested to Washington that it would be wise to have Catholic missioners working among the frontier tribes to "effect the civilization of the Indians" and of "attaching them to the interest of the United States," the president had gone before Congress and obtained subsistence funds for priests working among the Illinois Indians.

Bishop Carroll gave great encouragement to Mother

Elizabeth Seton. He had first heard of the New York widow and convert through mutual friends, the Filicchi brothers, Italian exporters in Leghorn and prominent Catholics. At the suggestion of Antonio Filicchi, Bishop Carroll had written to Mrs. Seton, encouraging her conversion. It was Antonio who also informed the bishop that the future St. Elizabeth Ann Seton had entered the Church with her five children. The bishop told his Italian friend that he would contribute toward the education of Mrs. Seton's sons. He met Mrs. Seton when he went to New York and found her among those who were to receive the sacrament of confirmation. From then on there was a regular correspondence between the two. Bishop Carroll approved a plan suggested by Father Louis William Dubourg, rector of St. Mary's Seminary, that she come to Baltimore and open a school. Bishop Carroll encouraged her in the foundation of her religious community, the Sisters of Charity of St. Joseph, and — although he was disappointed when she moved her headquarters from Baltimore to Emmitsburg — he continued to support what he considered a completely American enterprise.

In building the Church in America, Bishop Carroll realized that the help of religious orders was necessary. He encouraged a Franciscan foundation in Philadelphia only to have it fail. The Trappists tried to settle in Kentucky but withdrew. The bishop, however, was not one to give up. Two Augustinians from Ireland arrived in 1796, and although Bishop Carroll would have preferred them to take up work on the frontier, he supported them when they chose Philadelphia. The following year he could convey to them the good news that Rome had approved their establishment of a Philadelphia monastery, out of which was to grow Villanova University. The bishop was more persuasive with the Dominicans who came next. He sent them to Father Stephen Badin on the Kentucky frontier.

The Church in the United States was developing. Rome heard Bishop Carroll's plea and appointed Leonard Neale as his coadjutor; but the coadjutor, busy with Georgetown College and a community of women he was organizing, was of little help to Bishop Carroll who had a vast territory to cover. Wondering whether Rome had an appreciation of American geography, Bishop Carroll proposed four new dioceses to Rome: Boston, comprising the five states of New England; New York, which would cover the whole of New York state and northern New Jersey; Philadelphia, taking up the rest of New Jersey and all of Pennsylvania and Delaware; Bardstown, composed of Kentucky and Tennessee. He also sent along his recommendations of bishops for these posts. On April 8, 1808, Rome announced the American reorganization. Baltimore would become an archdiocese with four suffragan sees — Boston, New York, Philadelphia, and Bardstown. Bishops were appointed respectively: John Cheverus, Richard Luke Concanen, Michael Egan, and Benedict Flaget; in addition, the Holy See named Father Charles Nerinckx administrator for the Louisiana territory.

Bishop Carroll's declining years were made happy with the restoration of the Jesuits. He had no plans to take up his old vocation, but he was certain that the restored society would flourish in the United States. The War of 1812 caused the postponement of a planned provincial council. Bishop Carroll defended the conduct of President James Madison in the war and although the British blockade of Baltimore cut communications with Rome, it

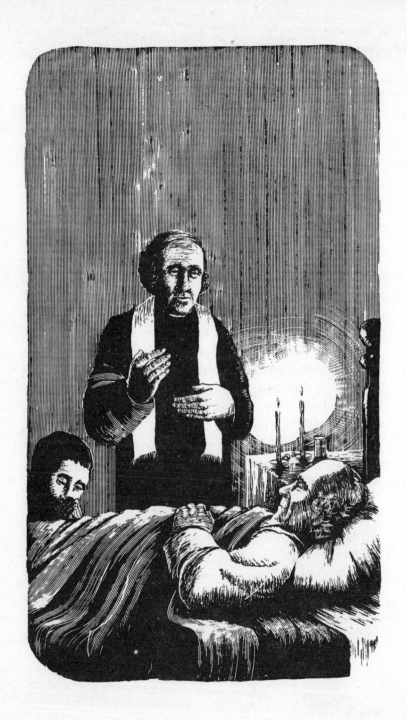

was the actual siege of the city in 1814 that made the war very real. The nearly eighty-year-old bishop was shaken when the British entered Washington to burn and loot. When in February of 1815 the Treaty of Ghent ended the war, like other Baltimoreans, the bishop enjoyed the "fireworks and illuminations" and "every demonstration of joy."

It was his last big joy. The bishop's tired body was wearing down and as the year progressed, his friends began to fear that the end was approaching. Mother Seton received a letter with fifty dollars from the bishop and knew he was weakening badly when she could barely decipher his scrawl. When Bishop Leonard Neale came from Georgetown on November 22, he recognized the presence of death. The next day, with the seminarians from St. Mary's kneeling about his bed, the bishop received the last rites. He spoke to the seminarians: "To all appearances, I shall shortly appear before my God and my Judge. Entreat His infinite mercy to forgive me my sins." Later he said, "Ah, if anyone should be lost through my fault, beg heaven to forgive me." He placed his confidence in God and commended himself to the Blessed Mother.

Bishop Carroll was to last for over a week more. On Sunday, December 3, 1815, with his sister Elizabeth at his side and other friends kneeling in the room, he urged them all to eat something and take a bit of rest. He lifted his arm and blessed them all, then he turned his face to the wall. The founder of the American Church was dead.

# CHAPTER 5

## *Father of California*

### *Junípero Serra*

Quite a few years ago, before the coming of the super-highways, I followed the narrow road that ran north from San Diego to San Francisco. I made the journey not to see the spectacular wonders of California but to retrace the path of a humble friar and to visit the string of missions he had founded. The trail that he pioneered was known as El Camino Real — The King's Highway — and as I drove northward I pictured a small man, five feet two inches, a fringe of hair above his round face, pleasantly featured, with a stockiness that could become pudgy, making the same journey but by foot. Dressed in the faded and dusty robe of a Franciscan friar, he herded before him cows, goats, pigs, and chickens. His only defense was a large crucifix and to everyone he met he had one greeting, brought with him from the Old World, *"Amar a Dios!"* — "Love God!" Who was he? His best biographer, Omer Englebert, titled his work *The Last of the Conquistadors: Junípero Serra*, and it is the only thing about the book that I do not like. This humble Franciscan was far from being a conqueror. Serra came to the New World not to rule but to serve. He journeyed ever northward, not to win lands but to civilize. The conquistadors were rapacious men of steel, quick to enslave, prone to punish; Serra was a man of love. The conquistadors were men of the flesh; Serra died wearing a hairshirt.

When President Calvin Coolidge set up a memorial to the founders of our nation, Junípero Serra was nominated by the state of California. His bronze bust stands in our nation's Capitol, right hand high with a crucifix, left hand balancing a California mission. Carved into the black marble base in letters of gold is the simple legend:

JUNIPERO SERRA

CALIFORNIA

Junípero Serra is all the more remarkable because he did not commence what has come to be regarded as his lifework until he was fifty-six years old and not in the most robust of health. At a time when many are thinking of slowing down or retiring, he began what would have been more than ambitious for a young man. It was as if all that went before was but preparation for the building of a state.

Junípero Serra was born at Petra on the island of Majorca on November 24, 1713, and baptized the same day as Miguel José Serre (he later adopted the Catalan spelling, Serra). His father, Antonio, was a laborer, working sometimes on farms, other times in a local quarry. His parents were religious people, belonging to the Franciscan Third Order. Because his father was close to the Franciscans, they accepted his son in their school and gave the boy a primary and classical education. He applied for admission to the Franciscan community in Palma but was turned down because of his height and frail appearance. The friars in Petra came to his support, spoke highly of his religiosity and intelligence, and their active support led to his acceptance. After a year of probation he was allowed to make his religious profession on September 15, 1731, and took as his new name, Junípero, after Brother Juniper, the faithful companion of Francis of Assisi. Serra, ordained in 1738, always considered his religious profession the happiest day in his life because "all good things came to me with it." He spent the next seventeen years at the Franciscan seminary in Palma, the first six studying philosophy and theology, two in graduate studies, and the balance teaching as a doctor of theology. Because of his learning and oratorical skills, he was in great demand as a preacher; but as he confided to his closest friend, Francisco Palou (who would be his first biographer), his greatest desire was to be a missioner and convert souls to Christ.

It did not seem as if this would be possible. Serra's superiors in Palma had expended great effort in his education, and he occupied an important position in their future plans because of the high regard given him in university circles. However, toward the end of 1748 a recruiter came from Mexico to seek personnel for San Fernando College there. Serra heard of the mission and told Francisco Palou that they ought to enlist. He knew his provincial would reject the idea, so he wrote directly to the commissioner general of the Indies who, acting for the king, had the final say in the matter. The request made by Fathers Serra and Palou was approved, and the two priests left for Cádiz where they prepared for the long journey to Veracruz, Mexico. Junípero Serra wrote a last letter to his parents, whom he never would see again, hoping to resign them to his separation.

On August 29, 1749, Serra, Palou, and some other missioners left Cádiz aboard a ship bound for New Spain. Travel in those days was not easy. Not only were quarters cramped and lacking in privacy, but fresh food did not last long. On this journey water ran low and the passengers were limited to half a pint a day. "There were moments my throat was burning so, I would have drunk slime," Serra wrote. "I have observed the best way of saving one's saliva is to eat little and talk still less." The ship finally made Puerto Rico, where it put into San Juan to replenish its supplies. The Franciscans used the opportunity to preach a mission, spending much time in the confessionals. "We went into them as early as three or four o'clock in the morning and remained there until midnight," he wrote a cousin who was also a priest. The ship left Puerto Rico, but as it neared Veracruz it ran into a storm. For three days the travelers were tossed about while the ship seemed to be breaking up under them and the pumps were unable to keep up with the flooding. Crew members begged the captain to beach the boat so that some might be saved. The Franciscans prayed to St. Barbara, the storm broke, and — when they reached Veracruz in January of 1750 — they offered a high Mass of thanksgiving to the saint, at which Mass Father Serra preached. All that remained was the two-week walk to Mexico City. It was during this trek that an accident befell Junípero Serra that would affect him for the rest of his life. While asleep he was bitten on the left foot by a scorpion. The poison spread up his leg and left him lame. The infection would break out at intervals, particularly after much walking.

San Fernando College was reached January 1, 1750. The purpose of this college was the evangelization and conversion of the Indian population. Serra was appointed prefect and directed to lead a group of missioners nearly two hundred miles northwest of Mexico City to work among the Pame Indians, a dissolute tribe that often left its mountain villages to raid haciendas. It was Serra's task to civilize them. He began by learning their language and translating the catechism and liturgical texts into their tongue. Then he had to teach them to read. He set up an agricultural economy, showing the Pames how to farm and raise livestock. Serra later remarked, "It was through their stomachs that the faith entered their heads." At any rate, the mission was successful, and after ten years the Franciscans could be withdrawn and the archbishop of Mexico City was able to replace them with his own priests.

Serra and Palou had been with the Pames for over eight years when they were recalled to go to Texas and work among the Apaches, to take the place of two Franciscans who had been murdered by the Indians. However, the Spanish troops who had been sent north to subdue the Apaches were instead defeated by a combined force of Apaches and Comanches. It was decided to delay the mission. Father Palou went back to the Pames as prefect, while Father Serra became an itinerant missioner, traveling through the dioceses of Mexico, Guadalajara, Puebla, Oaxaca, and Valladolid, and preaching missions of spiritual renewal.

The year 1767 was a decisive one for Junípero Serra. It not only marked his fifty-fourth birthday but was the year he began a new career. It came about because of the suppression of the Jesuits (which is another story in itself). On April 2 of that year Charles III of Spain ordered the Jesuits expelled from all the territory under the Spanish crown. When the news reached Mexico, the Jesuits there — numbering one hundred seventy-eight — were arrested and exiled to Corsica. (In 1773 Pope Clement XIV would suppress the Society of Jesus throughout the world.) Among the missions that the Jesuits had staffed in Mexico were those of Lower California. The minister for the Indies, José Galvez, ordered the friars of San Fernando to take responsibility for those missions. The result was that a band of sixteen monks was gathered and assigned to Baja California under the leadership of Junípero Serra as prefect and Francisco Palou as vice-prefect. There were fifteen mission stations along the length of the thousand-mile peninsula and this meant that until recruits could be found, each man would have to live alone. Serra, the six-teenth man, would be on the move most of the time. The Franciscans found the missions in a deplorable state. The soldiers who had been left to guard them after the removal of the Jesuits had looted them and had decimated the live-stock for food.

Serra and his missioners set about rebuilding and consolidating, but a new problem arose. Russian ships had been seen sailing along the Pacific coast of the penin-sula. Was the power of Spain to be challenged? It had been in the mind of the Spanish crown to settle the west coast of New Spain all the way to Alaska, but pacification and lack of manpower had only enabled missions to be es-tablished as far as Santa María, about three quarters of the way up the peninsula and some three hundred miles south of the present Mexican-American border. Serra met with the minister for the Indies and the two men developed a plan to settle Upper California, which the Spanish decreed began at the thirtieth parallel. In this largely unknown land Serra suggested that ten missions be built, one every fifty miles, so that no priest would be more than a two-day journey from his neighbors. But because there was nothing between Santa María and the border, five missions would have to be established in this unconquered area. It was decided that three northern missions would be founded at once to secure Upper California — one called San Diego would be just north of the border; one named after St. Bonaventure would be near the Santa Barbara Channel; and the last, named San Carlos Borromeo, would be on a bay which old maps listed as Monterey. Then came the logistics. Three ships were found to take the landing parties. Since these ships covered twelve to thirteen miles a day, it would take about two months for the first to reach San Diego. Meanwhile, land parties would be formed to drive north the livestock and poultry which would support the missions and be the basis for domesticating and civilizing the Indians.

Before each ship sailed, Father Serra went aboard to offer Mass, preach a sermon of exhortation, and give everyone the opportunity to go to confession. No one knew what lay ahead, and all wanted to be prepared. When the ships were gone, Serra began his own journey north on Easter Sunday, 1769. His first stop was with his friend Francisco Palou, at San Javier. The reason Serra gave in his journal was "to acquaint him with the work I was leaving to him as my successor." But undoubtedly it was also a matter of friendship, for Serra stayed three days with Palou. "I had never found him so ill," Palou recorded in his own diary. "There were running sores on his leg and foot. I begged him to let me go in his place, but he would not hear of it." When Serra was ready to leave, two men had to lift him into the saddle on his mule. It took more than a month for Father Serra to reach the last mission and go to the camp north of it where the land expedition was forming. At this camp he planted a cross and announced he was founding his first mission, calling it San Fernando de Velicatá and leaving a priest in charge.

On Trinity Sunday the expedition set out. There were twenty-five soldiers on horseback, thirty Indians from missions to the south (laborers and sappers to clear the road), one hundred seventy pack mules, and several hundred cows. The way was uncharted and they had to be guided by an astrolabe, an instrument eventually replaced by the sextant. Scouts went ahead to find water and pasture. Some of the mission Indians deserted along the way and some hostile Indians were met, but the soldiers had only to fire their guns in the air and the hostiles disappeared. The expedition members reached the bay on which the San Diego mission was to be founded on July 1. They saw two of the ships — *San Carlos* and *San Antonio* — lying at anchor; but the news was bad. Plague had broken out and thirty-one sailors were dead. The third ship had been shipwrecked and all aboard were lost. There were enough sailors left for one crew, so the *San Antonio* was sent back to Mexico for more men and supplies. An advance party under Captain Gasparde Portolá went ahead to claim the Monterey region.

On July 16, 1769, Father Junípero Serra planted a cross on a hill three miles from the harbor, offered Mass, and the mission of San Diego was founded — the first in present-day California. A stockade was built, a crude chapel erected, some cabins constructed for the friars, and two large tents were set up as quarantine hospitals to contain the thirty-five plague victims. In the days that followed, a cemetery was begun to bury nineteen more who would die. Indians attacked the camp, but the soldiers held them off. The weeks turned into months, and still nothing was heard from the *San Antonio* or from Portolá's column. "It is freezing here. My underclothes are in rags," Serra recorded. Then on January 24, 1770, Portolá returned. He had not found Monterey but had discovered another harbor farther north which he had named San Francisco. He said that the old Spanish maps were wrong. Monterey Bay simply did not exist; where it was supposed to be, a creek made its way into the open sea of a wide bay. Portolá, who held civil authority on the expedition, noted that they were down to eating old mules. He decided that the expedition would return to Velicatá if the *San Antonio* did not return by March 19. Father Serra replied that he would not retreat but remain behind. Father Juan Crespi volunteered to stay with him.

The days passed. Father Serra began a novena to St. Joseph which was finished on the evening of his feast. There was no sign of the ship. The next day, March 19 (the feast of St. Joseph), Serra offered Mass and preached a sermon on hope. Portolá made preparations for departure the next day. Just as dusk was falling, a sail appeared at the mouth of the harbor. It was the *San Antonio*. Thus by only hours the California project was saved. Moreover, the *San Antonio* had been instructed to go directly to Monterey but had lost its anchor and had decided to stop at San Diego and get an anchor from the *San Carlos*. The captain of the *San Antonio* insisted that Monterey existed and that the charts were correct. Portolá decided to try again and Father Serra said he would go with the *San Antonio*. On June 13 Serra was to write Palou, "This is indeed the famous harbor discovered by [Sebastián] Vizcaíno in 1603. As for saying why the first

77

expedition did not find it, that is not my affair. The great thing is that we are here."

Under the large oak where Vizcaíno's chaplain had celebrated the first Mass in California one hundred sixty-seven years earlier, Father Serra offered Mass anew. Bells had been hung from the tree and they rang out as a great cross was blessed and erected. The ceremony was not without sadness because at the foot of the cross a cabin boy who had died aboard the *San Antonio* was buried, a reminder that the advance of civilization was not without human cost. There was another problem that troubled Father Serra at this time. The presidio at Monterey was under the command of Lieutenant Pedro Fages, a crude and loathsome man, who embodied the vices that the English "Black Legend" attributed to all Spaniards. He beat and starved his soldiers, stole the best rations for his own use, and hindered the work of Father Serra at every chance. "How many times," Serra wrote to Palou, "I have thought his bullyings would be the death of me."

While Serra recognized the civil power, he did not wish to be too closely allied to it. Hence, he decided to move the Monterey mission away from the presidio. The spot he chose was on a stream three miles away that Vizcaíno had named Carmel. It was not only a beautiful spot but also had land suitable for farming and livestock breeding. Serra's description of this mission was typical of the others he built: "It is enclosed by a stockade 225 x 150 feet. The mission consists of three buildings: in the first are the kitchens; in the second the dormitory for young girls; in the third Father Crespi's room and mine, the temporary chapel, an office, the Indians' great hall and finally the storeroom, which alone measures 107 feet in length.

Backing up against the surrounding wall but outside it are the barracks, completely protected by a stockade made, like our own, of thick and very tall poles. Nearby are the corral, the vegetable garden and the cabins of the Indians." Carmel became Father Serra's favorite mission. He made it his headquarters and home. It must be remembered that California was virgin territory and the Franciscans had to be self-reliant. They had to build forges, tanneries, grain mills, wineries, carpentry shops, brickyards; in short, they manufactured what they needed.

The problem with Fages came to a head by the middle of 1772. His cruel ways had caused many soldiers to desert, but he blamed this on the padres. He was preventing the opening of new missions. He was intercepting mail to the priests. Despite the fact that he was in ill health, Junípero Serra concluded that he had to go to Mexico and make matters known. Fages forbade Serra to leave and he ordered the captain of the *San Carlos* not to allow the priest aboard. Both the priest and the ship's captain ignored the commandant and, on October 20, the *San Carlos* sailed with Father Serra aboard. Favorable winds made the trip unusually short, fifteen days to reach San Blas. Father Serra was accompanied by Juan Evangelista — a teenage Indian boy who served as his interpreter — and the two began the very long journey to Mexico City. At Guadalajara they came down with fever. Father Serra was given the last rites, or extreme unction (as the sacrament of the anointing of the sick used to be called); but he was more concerned about the Indian boy entrusted to his care. In time, both recovered and they set out again. They walked the two hundred miles to Queretaro where Serra was stricken again. The last rites were ordered again for him; but before they could be given, Serra made one of those sudden recoveries which were typical of him. A few days later they resumed their walk to Mexico City, a hundred miles away.

The viceroy of Mexico at this time was Antonio María Bucareli y Ursúa, an honest and moral man, who was both a good Christian and a loyal Spaniard. He received Father Serra at once. "He was half-dying when I saw him arrive here," Bucareli wrote in a report. "The apostolic flame that burned in him made an extraordinary impression on me. It was his opinions and his desires which gave inspiration for my decisions." Bucareli knew that Upper California would not exist without Serra and that he alone had kept the original expedition from retreat, so he listened carefully to what the priest had to say. Serra told him that the venture was in trouble but that it could be saved. "If you remove the obstacles which I point out to you, and grant the assistance for which I beg," stated Serra, "we shall make of these pagan tribes a great Christian people, and of their land the most beautiful of all the king's colonies." The viceroy told the priest to prepare a document that they could both submit to the government cabinet. Junípero Serra went back to San Fernando and prepared a long memorandum of nine thousand words, consisting of thirty-two articles.

Among the points Serra made in this document were the following: Fages should be replaced; any soldier who abuses the Indians should be removed from the mission; the responsibility for educating and directing the Indians belongs solely to the missioners; except for capital crimes, neither commandant nor soldiers can punish Indians without consultation with the priests; the capital of the newly conquered territory be removed from Loreto in Baja California to Monterey; supplies for the priests should go to them directly and not through the commandant; a new frigate should be completed to bring supplies and end the famines; blacksmiths and carpenters should be sent to teach their trades to the Indians; a doctor is needed in Monterey; with the arrival of a new commandant, an amnesty be given those who deserted; soldiers who marry Indian women should be given a plot of ground, two cows and a mule, and allowed to remain at the mission where they married; that no commandant be allowed to open or delay letters sent to the missioners; that the cows meant for the missions of Santa Clara and San Francisco be taken from the commandant at Monterey and given to the mission which can use the milk for the Christian children. There were many other points. At the meeting with the viceroy and his cabinet Father Serra explained his document and it was approved with some minor changes. At last, the missioner believed, his work would be on solid footing.

Bucareli gave Father Serra the equivalent of $25,000 — and the priest delayed his return for two months to regain his health and purchase supplies. He also recruited workmen and their families. The delay also allowed the frigate *Santiago* — which had twice the tonnage of the *San Carlos* and *San Antonio* together — to be completed at San Blas. After unloading its cargo (consisting of Serra's recruits and supplies) at San Diego and Monterey, the brand-new *Santiago* was to go north and explore new lands for Spain. During the seven weeks it took to reach San Diego, one of Father Serra's workman-recruits died and was buried at sea. Father Palou notes that Father Serra returned in much better condition than when he had left. The news that Serra brought back was good and the missioners saw that their work could expand. About this time also came the discovery that an overland route had been found between Mexico and Upper California. For years it had been assumed that no direct connection existed. Now, after considerable agony, a party of Spanish explorers had pioneered a land route that would save time and money and avoid the perils of the sea.

The years that followed were a time of great building. New recruits came from Mexico to swell Franciscan ranks. The original plan that Serra drew up was to establish nineteen missions. Father Serra was to start nine of these (whose full names are shown here): San Diego de Alcalá (1769); San Carlos Borromeo (1770); San Antonio de Padua and San Gabriel Arcángel (1771); San Luís Obispo de Tolosa (1772); San Juan Capistrano and San Francisco de Asís (Palou under Serra's direction) (1776); Santa Clara de Asís (1777); and San Buenaventura (1782).

The settlements of Los Angeles and Santa Barbara were also founded in Serra's lifetime. After his death twelve additional missions were begun, bringing the total number to twenty-one. These — again listed according to their full names — are: Santa Barbara (1786); La Purísima Concepcíon (1787); Santa Cruz and Nuestra Señora de la Soledad (1791); San José de Guadalupe, San Juan Bautista, San Miguel Arcángel, and San Fernando Rey de España (1797); San Luís Rey de Francia (1798); Santa Inés (1804); San Rafael Arcángel (1817); and San Francisco Solano (1823).

In many ways the California missions were similar to the Jesuit reductions in Paraguay. As touched on in Chapter 3, the reductions (or resettlement communities) were the great social experiments of the New World. The missioners had their own dreams of Utopia and they set about building ideal civilizations in both South America and North America. In each instance the missioners went among a primitive and savage people whom they turned into artisans and artists. They trained the natives in how to grow crops and raise livestock and thus end their nomadic and uncertain hunting. These Indians had never seen a nail, a horse, or a plank. They knew nothing of tools or wheels. Yet under the guidance of the padres they built cathedrals in the wilderness. They learned to read and write, to sing plain chant, to paint and sculpture. The great tragedy is that both experiments ended suddenly — the southern reductions disappearing with the suppression of the Jesuits, the California missions pillaged in the overthrow of Spain by Mexican anticlericals.

Moreover, what was done in California was done without force or compulsion. Father Serra was a great respecter of the rights of the Indians. He ruled that the Indians had to come to the mission of their own free will. When a group of Indians — in the early days — attacked the San Diego mission and killed the Franciscan padre there, Father Serra obtained amnesty for the culprits. The Indians were also free to leave at will.

It was the Indians under the mission guidance who planted and harvested the orange trees, the olive trees, the grapevines. It was the Indians who dug the canals for irrigation, who built bridges over streams, who sculptured the road from San Diego to San Francisco. A visitor to the missions wrote: "Everything is a pretext for enjoyment. . . . It is a festivity for the women to go and wash the linen in common, to eat together under the trees, then to come home at night in the big ox-carts, singing beneath the stars. . . . It is another festival for the men who, when the harvest is finished, bring home the last heads of grain braided together in the form of a cross and go in procession and place them on the altar." Another visitor summed up what he saw: "It is the return of the Golden Age."

Around the missions Serra planned, grew the great cities of California — San Diego, Los Angeles, Ventura, Santa Barbara, Monterey, Santa Clara, San Francisco. The road that he laid out provided for the commerce between these cities. The crops that he introduced brought great wealth to the state of California. Mission architecture is today reproduced all over the state and has become a symbol for the Golden West.

Of all the missions he built, San Carlos Borromeo at Carmel — as mentioned earlier — was Father Serra's favorite. It was the second mission erected and the area he chose for it is one of the most picturesque in the entire United States. From the beginning he made it his headquarters, roughly halfway between San Diego and San Francisco. The mission was built in the shape of a quadrangle. In the center of the quadrangle was a fountain to provide water for drinking, cooking, and for the workshops which stood opposite the church which Serra had designed in remembrance of churches he had known on Majorca, particularly in its Moorish dome. The church decorations are notable for their hardwoods, not available in the area (Serra had asked that supplies from Mexico be sent in crates of hardwood which he could then use in building). In the monastery which ran down one side of the square,

Serra had his office and his cell — a small room with one window, a wooden pallet to sleep upon, a chair, and a small table. In the monastery was the first library in California, seven hundred volumes sent up from San Fernando in Mexico, discards from the library there. It was a house to which missioners could come from other posts for rest and spiritual rejuvenation.

The missions were in a sense pure communism with everything held in common. They embraced vast tracts of land, the boundaries being the borders of the next mission. They possessed on an average ten thousand head of cattle, twelve thousand sheep, one thousand horses, several thousand goats and pigs, and uncounted chickens — all descended from a few pairs of ancestors brought in during the first days. Each year a mission would harvest about twelve thousand bushels of grain. About a thousand to fifteen hundred Indians lived within hearing of the church bell. From the central storeroom the Indians received their daily rations and their weekly allotment of meat. From the same storeroom they withdrew clothing as they needed it, clothing they themselves had made. The mission hospital took care of the ill. Nearby was a communal cemetery.

There are those who say that the reductions and the California missions were nothing but paternalism and as such should be condemned. They forget that at their stage of development the Indians needed paternalism. Serra and his companions had as their goal the conversion of the Indians, to bring them to Christ. "All my life I have wanted to be a missioner," Serra said on Majorca when he was applying to go to New Spain. "I have wanted to carry the Gospel teachings to those who have never heard of God and the kingdom He has prepared for them. But I became proud and allowed myself to be distracted by academic studies. Now I am filled with remorse that my ambition has been so long delayed." Serra and his friars wanted nothing for themselves but everything for their Indians. They found a people annihilating one another in cannibalistic rituals and brought them into the peace of Christ. They integrated the Indian into their own society and did not destroy him as did the advancing Anglo-Saxons. Those who saw the California missions firsthand — and many of these witnesses were neither Catholic nor Spanish — had nothing but admiration for the work of the padres. It took later generations who never saw the missions to produce some who could be critical.

Serra realized the accomplishments he set out to do despite a never-robust health. He refused to be incapacitated by his bad leg and thought nothing of the thousand-mile round trip to visit his missions. Thus 1784 found him seventy-one years old but still tireless. In January he returned to Carmel from San Diego where he had gone to bestow the sacrament of confirmation, a privilege given him that was usually reserved to bishops. In April he traveled to Santa Clara and San Francisco to again confirm. He had great expectations for this latter mission, writing some years earlier, "The famous port of Monterey is nothing compared to what that of our Father St. Francis will become." Returning from the Bay area, he stopped again at Santa Clara to consecrate the new church and make his retreat, at the end of which he made a general confession. He told a shocked Father Palou that he was preparing for death.

In June he was back at his beloved Carmel. Those

who knew him recognized that his strength was failing. The congestion in his lungs caused him long spells of coughing and weakness. He was planning the establishment of two new missions — Santa Barbara and La Purísima Concepción — and he was disappointed that the latest supply ship brought no new priests to staff them. On August 8 he wrote his superior at San Fernando asking that he petition for more friars; but in this, his last letter, thoughts of death were not too far away. He also wrote, "I have suffered deeply in the death of so many of our Brothers," and he concludes that he is waiting for the Immaculate Lady "to open heaven's door to us." By mid-August he had taken to his bed. His friend Captain Canizares, who had taken him aboard his ship when he made the journey to find justice against Pedro Fages, arrived in Monterey. When he heard that Serra was very ill, he sent the ship's doctor to Carmel. The doctor prescribed that red-hot irons be applied to the sick man's chest. Father Serra allowed the torture to take place.

On August 26 Junípero Serra dragged himself to the chapel to receive Holy Communion for the last time. Francisco Palou had offered to bring the sacrament to him, but Serra had replied, "It is not for Our Lord to leave His place for me, but for me to go to Him." Afterward, he called for the mission carpenter and gave instructions on building him a simple coffin. He asked Palou to anoint him and he received the oils sitting in his chair. The next day Captain Canizares called on him and Serra greeted his old friend: "How good you are to have come back from so far away to throw a handful of dirt upon my head!" The next day he arose and sat in a chair to recite his breviary. Since it was after the noon hour, he drank a cup of broth.

Then he asked to be helped back to his pallet where he lay down on his bed fully dressed. Thus he passed from this life at a quarter to two on the afternoon of August 28, 1784.

Father Palou came in and took off the hairshirt Father Serra always wore. He helped lay the body in its coffin. The Indians came bearing field flowers and weeping at the loss of El Viejo, The Old One. They stayed with the body all night, reciting the rosary. The next day Father Palou said the Mass of burial and afterward the body was laid in a tomb at the left of the altar. "The weeping of the congregation drowned out the voices of the singers," Palou wrote. As the Indians began to leave the chapel, they broke out in singing the "Alabado," a hymn El Viejo had taught them. It was their last tribute to one who had truly been their spiritual father and the Father of California.

# CHAPTER 6

## *Tarheel Apostle*

### *Thomas Frederick Price*

When does a Church come of age? From its beginning until 1908 the Church in the United States was considered a mission-receiving Church, under the jurisdiction of the mission arm of the universal Church, the Congregation of Propaganda (today's Sacred Congregation for the Evangelization of Peoples and the Propagation of the Faith). When independence from England came, there was hardly more than a handful of priests in the Thirteen Colonies, yet at the same time Catholic immigration from Europe was growing. In the beginning, French priests — exiled by the revolution in their homeland — came to U.S. shores. These were followed by a large number of Irish clergy. When immigration began from northern Europe, German and Polish priests followed; then, as Italian waves reached America, priests from Italy arrived to care for their people. So to answer when a Church comes of age, it would seem that the minimum requirement would be when that Church can care for its own needs. However, for many students of Church history, a Church only comes of age when it begins to send its own sons and daughters to assist needy Churches to become established in other and distant parts of the world.

As the twentieth century began, there was no mission movement in the United States, and when jurisdiction of the United States — in 1908 — was removed from Propaganda to the congregations handling the established Churches, it was as if the Holy See was saying, "You are now grown up. Go help others." One man who heard this voice was a North Carolina priest, and from his response came a great American mission movement.

Thomas Frederick Price was born in Wilmington, North Carolina, on August 19, 1860, a rare breed because he was a Catholic in a state where Catholics were few. His youth was spent in the shadow and aftermath of the Civil War. When Wilmington was attacked by Union forces, his family had to flee as refugees. They later returned only to survive a yellow-fever plague that claimed a fifth of the city's population. The end of the Civil War brought even greater woes as the carpetbaggers moved in to exploit the defeated people. Cruel restrictions were placed upon the citizens. There were shortages of every kind of goods, and people had to sell their heirlooms at low prices to Northern exploiters simply to exist.

When Fred (as young Thomas Frederick Price was called) was eight years old, North Carolina was split from the diocese of Charleston (South Carolina) and set up as a new vicariate (the future diocese of Raleigh). Appointed vicar apostolic of the new region was a Baltimore priest, Father James Gibbons, later to become a cardinal and the leading American churchman. Father Gibbons was consecrated a bishop and he chose Fred's parish, St. Thomas, as his headquarters. Fred was an altar boy and not only served the new bishop's Mass but also came to know him well, a fact that would be instrumental years later when Father Price went to Cardinal Gibbons for help.

When he reached sixteen, Fred Price announced that he wished to become a priest. It was not an easy decision.

His father, a newspaper editor, had died four years earlier and Fred's after-school jobs helped his widowed mother. However, Clarissa Price was a woman used to making sacrifices and she encouraged her son. Both she and her husband had been converts to the Catholic Church and, like so many converts, she was a person of great zeal and charity. Her own Christian example could very well have been the inspiration for her son's choice.

Arrangements were made for Fred to enter St. Charles Preparatory Seminary in Baltimore that September. In those days the easiest way to reach Baltimore was by ship. So in early fall Fred Price boarded the *Rebecca Clyde* for the journey north. The ship was off Portsmouth Bank, below Cape Hatteras, when a fierce storm struck. Waves crashed over the ship while the captain fought the storm trying to make Ocracoke Inlet and the relative safety of Pamlico Bay. Along with two other passengers, young Price lashed himself to the mainmast. Suddenly a huge wave struck the ship, the vessel keeled over, and Fred was washed into the raging sea. He could not swim and death seemed certain.

William O'Connell, a classmate (who was to become cardinal-archbishop of Boston), related in his own autobiography how he persuaded Fred to tell him what happened on that fateful day. Calling Price "this young saint," he gave this account: "Keeping his head as best he could, above the furious waters, he cried again, 'Christ Jesus, save me or I perish.' Like a flash the sky seemed to open, and out of a speck of blue came the clearest possible vision, as clear as he saw the howling waves about him — Mary, the Mother of Christ, appeared before his eyes. Upon her face was a smile, and, gently stretching forth

her hand, she pointed to a great floating plank which had been washed overboard from the sinking ship. Strengthened superhumanly by the perfect confidence of safety, he gained the plank, pulled himself upon it, threw himself face forward upon it and, grasping a great ring on its upper surface, he swung, now up, now down, in the great waves about him, feeling nothing and thinking now and then of the vision, which would always remain indelibly imprinted in his soul. He began the Litany of the Blessed Virgin and, as he said, 'In my joy I almost sang it.' "

Whatever he experienced on that fateful day profoundly affected his future life in which the Blessed Virgin was to be his closest confidant. In any event, his plank — like other flotsam — was finally cast up on the sands of Portsmouth Island, and it was there that some islanders found him. It was almost a week before he made his way back to Wilmington, bereft of all his possessions and with only the clothes on his back, and it was not until February of 1877 that he finally reached St. Charles to begin his studies. He passed next through St. Mary's, the major seminary, where he was taught by Sulpician Fathers to whom later he would often turn for advice and help, and he received his orders through the diaconate from his old mentor, James Gibbons (then archbishop of Baltimore). He was ordained a priest in his home parish in Wilmington in June of 1886.

Father Price was assigned to the oldest parish at New Bern. He was continually on the go, traveling by foot, buggy, and stagecoach. It was the task of Priest Price, as he came to be called, to make the Church known among people who had little use for it and whose heads were filled with anti-Catholic nonsense. Once, while riding in a stage, two women opposite him kept staring at him. Finally, one asked: "Are you a papist priest?" He replied: "I'm a Roman Catholic priest." More stares, then, "Is it true that papist priests have horns?" Father Price doffed his hat and bowed his head, "I'm only a young priest." All his encounters were not so humorous. There was a storekeeper who refused to sell to him when he learned that his customer was a priest. On another occasion, during a rainstorm, he was driven from the shelter of a house porch by its shotgun-toting owner who wanted no priests on his property. But there were those who listened and accepted his tracts.

He lectured and preached wherever he could. When he was moved to Raleigh in 1896, the paper there reported: "This gifted young North Carolinian is only thirty-five years old. He is a patriot to the heart's core, and is giving his life to preaching and teaching in his native state. He has lectured in Littleton, Oxford, Smithfield, Goldsboro, Raleigh, and Asheville, and is this week in Clinton."

As he traveled about, Price became convinced that three things were necessary. First, there was a need for a Catholic publication that would present the truths of the faith to fair-minded Protestants and at the same time strengthen the beliefs of Catholics. Second, there was the need for a missionary apostolate in North Carolina that would attract helpers from outside the state. Third, there were too many orphans wandering about homeless and some sort of a shelter was needed. Once he isolated the needs, he planned to do something about them.

The first problem he tackled was the publication. He decided in 1897 on a monthly magazine which he named

*Truth*. He raised enough money to publish a first issue of five hundred copies and trusted that once he began the project, Our Lady would see it through. His confidence was not misplaced. The magazine grew to a thousand, then twelve thousand, and at its height reached one hundred twenty thousand copies a month. It gained a national circulation and was the indirect parent of what was to become the Catholic weekly *Our Sunday Visitor*, published in Huntington, Indiana. It happened this way: In 1908, a young priest by the name of John Noll, pastor of Hartford City, Indiana, was facing many of the anti-Catholic problems that Father Price was meeting head-on. Noll found *Truth* to be a valuable tool in his apostolate. He made arrangements with Price for bulk subscriptions and then substituted his own cover (with the title *The Parish Monthly*) which gave local news and met local problems. In time Noll concluded he could publish his own magazine, so he dropped *Truth* and launched what eventually was to be called *The Family Digest*. A few years later, in 1912, Noll started *Our Sunday Visitor*, a weekly aimed at fighting the anti-Catholic publication called *The Menace*.

With *Truth* successfully launched, Price turned to the problems of orphans. Again without money, he left the problem up to the Blessed Virgin and began searching for a site. He found an ideal spot outside Raleigh, a hilltop looking down on North Carolina State College. Enough donations were found to purchase the six hundred acres which he named Nazareth. He made repairs to a large old house on the property, obtained five Sisters from Our Lady of Mercy Convent in Charleston, built a chapel, and soon had forty orphans. He began a new publication, *The Orphan Boy*, to support the project.

Father Price also saw the orphanage property as the location for his mission-training house. He realized that with the small number of Catholics in North Carolina he would have to go out of the state to get recruits. He erected a new building which he named Regina Apostolorum (Queen of the Apostles) and went north seeking recruits. The seminary opened in the fall of 1902 with twenty-five seminarians who would make their preliminary studies there and then go to Belmont Abbey for major seminary studies. Price also instituted another innovation. He persuaded Northern seminarians to spend their summer vacations at Nazareth, doing field work as missioners. During this period he was also busy building rural chapels to serve as the center of his missionary preaching.

One of the great mysteries of this period is how Price supported his work. He had no large fund-raising operation, and — although everything was spartan and without frills — his work was a considerable complex to finance. Seminarians and orphans did manual labor each day to care for the upkeep of the place, and there were gardens to grow vegetables in season. In his travels outside the diocese, Price often spoke to raise funds for the work. Somehow, he kept it all going.

In the spring of 1904 there was to be an encounter that changed his life. During Easter week of that year a meeting of the Catholic Missionary Union was held in Washington, D.C., and Father Price was invited to speak on localized missions. Also on the program of the conference was a young priest from Boston, Father James Anthony Walsh, who was director there of the Society for the Propagation of the Faith. Walsh spoke on the need for the United States to become engaged in foreign mission work and he said that such an effort would not hurt home-mission efforts but would stimulate vocations for home needs. Price, during the question-and-answer period following the talk, supported the thesis of the speaker, and when the program ended he was introduced to the Boston priest. It was all quite casual and passing but was to have great future import for both men.

Father Price returned to North Carolina. He wrote about the meeting in *Truth*, calling missionary effort "the great work of the Church" and urging aid for the mission of the Society for the Propagation of the Faith. He asked God to speed the efforts of James Anthony Walsh. His writing in *Truth* took on a more universal note and it was obvious that the Washington meeting was frequently in his thoughts. But there were other things to occupy his mind. A tragic fire at Nazareth destroyed his seminary and one boy was killed in jumping to the ground. What he had worked so many years for was gone in a matter of hours. Undaunted, Price set about rebuilding and in a year a new fireproof Regina Apostolorum was opened.

Father Price's piety often led to misunderstandings and it made even some of those who were close to him uneasy. As is often the case, people suspect what they do not understand and they misinterpret a lifestyle that is different from their own. Price was sometimes accused of being impractical, and perhaps his dependence on the Blessed Virgin left realists cold; but the center he built at Raleigh and what he accomplished in North Carolina were not the work of an impractical man. That Thomas Frederick Price was a saintly man, no one would deny; but sanctity is not always appreciated by those who live with it. Price was indifferent to ordinary human concerns — food, shelter, a bit of ease. He went off to lonely places to kneel in prayer for long periods. He slept without a mattress; he wore a spiked chain around his waist that dug into his skin; he practiced mortifications and penances that others eschewed. During one retreat, he resolved to keep a diary that would consist of a letter each day to the Blessed Virgin, a resolve he kept until the end of his life.

The meeting in Washington had lifted Father Price's sights beyond North Carolina and the United States to the world. He began to question whether his vocation was limited to the Tarheel State or to fields beyond. Father Walsh had started a magazine in Boston, *The Field Afar*, and Father Price read it with growing conviction that what had been done at Nazareth should be repeated on an international scale. The matter was occupying his mind when he decided to attend the International Eucharistic Congress that was held in September of 1910 at Montreal. He, along with some other American priests, stayed in a convent where lodging was cheap. At breakfast one morning, someone happened to mention that he had seen James Anthony Walsh at the congress and then mentioned where Walsh was staying. At that moment the thoughts of the past several years came together and Price hurried to a phone. He reached Walsh, who was preparing to leave for the outdoor congress Mass at Fletcher Field, and the Boston priest promised to wait for him. Price was there within minutes. Walsh had been thinking along lines similar to Price's. He had made several inquiries about European mission societies establishing branches in the United States. A Paulist friend had suggested that the Boston priest start something himself. But Walsh felt that such a project should belong to the American hierarchy and he hesitated about personal involvement. Because time was pressing for the Mass, the Boston priest suggested that both men meet that night at the Windsor Hotel.

Thus the concept for the Catholic Foreign Mission Society of America was born on the evening of September 10, 1910, in a Canadian hotel. There was a meeting of minds between the two American priests. Father Price told of his experience in North Carolina and his plan for a society of secular priests who would live as a religious community in the work of the missions there. Father Walsh, who was familiar with the mission-sending societies of Europe, contributed that experience. Unfortunately, no minutes were ever kept of that meeting; but when the two priests departed for their own lodgings, it was agreed that groundwork should be laid. There is no question but that Price was the catalyst to get the movement going and what followed showed that he was the key to keeping it alive. The Montreal conversation was not going to be just talk. There were letters back and forth, as ideas took shape on paper.

Father Price went to see his boyhood friend James Gibbons, by this time a cardinal and recognized as the leader of the Catholic hierarchy. The cardinal — who had followed his former altar boy's career with interest and knew firsthand of the problems he had tackled — was supportive but told Father Price that a project of international scope would need the approval of the Holy See; so Father Price went to Washington to explain the plan to Archbishop Diomede Falconio, the apostolic delegate. The pope's representative replied that such a movement would be welcomed by the Holy See if it had the approval of the

American bishops. He suggested that a letter be sent to the archbishops telling of the project and asking for a discussion at their spring meeting. Back to Baltimore and Cardinal Gibbons went Father Price. The cardinal agreed to send out a letter to the archbishops asking if they approved the establishment of an American foreign mission society (that is, a seminary) and requesting suggestions as to its location. Price went to New York and gained the support of Archbishop John Farley, then to Boston to see his old classmate Archbishop William O'Connell; both archbishops were shortly to become cardinals.

There was a month between Cardinal Gibbons's letter to the archbishops and the spring meeting, and Price used the time to visit bishops who knew him and urge the project on them. He knew that these suffragans would be consulted by their respective archbishops for their opinions. On April 27, 1911, Price was at Catholic University waiting nervously outside the meeting room in Caldwell Hall as the archbishops discussed the project. He expected to be called to answer objections, but he had done the groundwork well and Cardinal Gibbons ably represented him. The project passed unanimously. A resolution was handed him which approved the founding of an American seminary for foreign missions. The resolution said in part: "We warmly commend to the Holy Father the two priests mentioned as organizers, and we instruct them to proceed to Rome without delay, for the purpose of securing all necessary authorization." Father Price hurried to send a telegram to Father Walsh in Boston; now that the groundwork was done he would look to the Boston priest to supervise the details while he prayed for success.

The two founders sailed for Rome at the end of

March. It was Price's first visit to the Holy City and he confided in his diary that here "I feel the concentration of God's authority." With the aid of the Mill Hill Fathers, whom Walsh knew, a petition was prepared for Propaganda. There were conferences with Cardinal Gotti, head of the congregation, and other officials. On June 29, 1911, both priests were summoned to meet with Cardinal Gotti. He told them the congregation approved their request, that they were authorized to purchase property and recruit students; the American foreign mission seminary was thus established. Since it was the feast of St. Peter and St. Paul, both priests felt that their foundation day was most auspicious. The cardinal told them that an audience with Pope Pius X was arranged for the next day. Father Price presented the pope with a bound volume of *Truth*, and Father Walsh gave the pontiff a bound volume of *The Field Afar*. The pope autographed a picture of himself, giving his blessing to the founders, their new society, and the society's benefactors.

The founders did not return home immediately. James Anthony Walsh planned on visiting other mission institutes and learning from them. Thomas Frederick Price wanted to go to Lourdes — to which he had great devotion — and make a retreat there. Although it had been agreed that Walsh would be the superior of the new society, Price was selected to write to his friend Cardinal Gibbons and break the good news. He told the cardinal that both he and Walsh agreed that the cardinal should have the honor of naming the new group. "We would suggest," he wrote, "The Catholic Foreign Mission Society of America." It was a name Walsh had coined, and when the cardinal approved of it, it became the official and legal title of the new society (although "Maryknoll" and "The Maryknoll Fathers" became the popular usage after the society purchased its first property and named the hill on which its seminary was to be erected, Mary's Knoll).

While Father Walsh went off on the practical matters of their foundation, Father Price hurried to Lourdes. He fell in love with the place and for the first time began to delve into the life of the peasant girl Bernadette Soubirous, to whom the Virgin had appeared and identified herself as "the Immaculate Conception." Price's spiritual diary tells of the profound effect both Lourdes and Bernadette had on him. He made a pilgrimage to Nevers where Bernadette had retired to become a nun and he spent a night kneeling before her tomb. Before he left Nevers, he arranged with the mother superior there that after his death his heart would be buried close to Bernadette. When he returned to America, he wrote the first English life of the young peasant girl and thus introduced her to Americans. From then on he signed his diary entries with the initials "M.B.," for the Mother of God, Mary, and "my little Sister," Bernadette.

When the two founders returned to the United States, they began a search for a headquarters. Both agreed it should be in the North and Father Walsh believed it should be close to New York City. Walsh had a friend — a Dominican missioner who had served in foreign fields — who was then pastor in Hawthorne, New York, and who suggested that Hawthorne would be an ideal place to begin. They approached Archbishop Farley of New York, who welcomed them into his diocese. Father Price went to North Carolina to turn his various projects over to priests who had assisted him. They had decided to use Walsh's

*Field Afar* for the new society while Price arranged for *Truth* to continue under other auspices.

The two priests found property at Hawthorne, but it was soon inadequate. A new site was located in Pocantico Hills, adjoining the estate of John D. Rockefeller, who when he heard of the transaction bought the property out from under them. They found a new site on a hill outside Ossining, New York, and Rockefeller — to avoid a suit — made a settlement which paid for the sewers of the new headquarters. It was a lovely site, overlooking the Hudson River. Father Walsh suggested that it be named after Mary, and Father Price happily consented. While Walsh organized the seminary, Price took to the road, visiting bishops and speaking, wherever he could get an invitation, for funds and recruits. He visited Bishop Michael Hoban in Scranton and received permission to open a preparatory seminary in that diocese. Walsh went to China to seek out a foreign mission for the new society, and the Paris Foreign Mission Society agreed to share a territory in South China.

The first mission group from Maryknoll was scheduled to leave for China early in September of 1918. Three young priests — James Edward Walsh (no relation to James Anthony Walsh), Bernard Meyer, and Francis X. Ford — were selected to pioneer the work, and Price volunteered to go as superior. He knew that Maryknoll was in capable hands and his thirty-two years of mission experience would be valuable to solve the problems and difficulties that might lie ahead. What he did not realize was that he was at an age when learning a new language would be difficult and mastering the intricacies of Chinese next to impossible.

The group arrived at their new mission on December 21. Father Price sent the news to Father Walsh, apologizing for not cabling because he thought fifteen dollars for a cable was too expensive. He wrote again after Christmas, describing the feast as celebrated at the mission. Price tried to learn the language, but he found it frustrating; and, as the months passed, he became more and more concerned that he would fail as a missioner. A tooth became ulcerated and it was decided that he should go to Hong Kong and see a dentist. On the trip to Hong Kong, he developed a severe pain in his side; so on reaching Hong Kong, he went to St. Paul's Hospital. The doctors diagnosed appendicitis and decided to operate. As he was prepared for surgery, the Sister making him ready wanted to remove the chains he had put about him, but they were padlocked and he had long since thrown away the keys. When the doctors opened him, they discovered that the appendix had burst and that he was full of gangrene. There was nothing they could do. Father Price died on September 12, 1919, the feast of the Holy Name of Mary; if he had been free to do so, he would have picked that feast day himself.

The society Thomas Frederick Price had helped found spread from China, around the world. Its missioners were to face death and exile. Two of the band he led to China would suffer at the hands of the Communists. Francis X. Ford would die from cruel neglect in a Red prison, and another jail would be the home of James Edward Walsh for many years. Since Father Price died so early in the history of Maryknoll, he is not always given the credit that James Anthony Walsh received. But his North Carolina years proved him a great missioner, and

Maryknoll stands as much his monument as anyone else's. His heart is at Nevers, France, and the rest of his remains at Maryknoll, New York, where a black marble tomb joins him forever with the remains of Bishop Walsh, his partner in making the Church of the United States come of age.

# *PART THREE*

## The Emigrés □ *INTRODUCTION*

While most American schoolchildren can identify the Marquis de Lafayette as a French soldier who helped George Washington, few Americans — children or adults — appreciate or give full credit to the contribution of the French in the establishment of the United States. It is quite possible that without French help the American War of Independence might not have been won by the Americans.

The French contributed thirty thousand soldiers, led by ninety officers, to the American cause. In 1780, Count Jean de Rochambeau (who later was named marshal of France during the French Revolution) was sent with six thousand soldiers under his command; from the time of his arrival that year until the final surrender of the British he was continually at the side of Washington. Admiral François de Grasse and his fleet of fifty-one ships forced the Royal Navy to retreat to New York and blockaded supplies from reaching the British general Cornwallis. The French presence swung the balance of power and led to the British surrender at Yorktown.

Likewise the American Church owes a great debt of

gratitude to the French. God often draws good out of evil. The French Revolution which was a tragedy for the Church in France became a blessing for the Church in the United States. The uprising which put many priests and nuns to death and closed Catholic institutions in France forced other priests to flee the country and take up work elsewhere. Sulpicians, skilled in the training of seminarians, came to the United States and established a seminary in Baltimore, a seminary which was the greatest single influence in the training of an American priesthood. Even when other seminaries were founded they were fashioned after the Sulpician model, and the Sulpician influence continues to this day. The French clergy who came to the United States were the salvation of the Catholic missions of the Midwest which were no longer being cared for by Quebec.

During the decade ending in 1800, twenty-seven French priests came to the United States, doubling the number of Catholic clergy. Diocese after diocese owes its beginning to French clergy whose names should long be cherished — Stephen Badin, Simon Bruté, Gabriel Richard, Benedict Flaget, John David, and Anthony Blanc, to mention but a few. These men were remarkable in that they were not castoffs who couldn't make the grade at home but were instead educated and cultured priests, many from well-to-do families, who freely chose to work in the American wilderness despite all the hardships, loneliness, and sacrifices such work entailed. They constantly had to appeal to French dioceses for financial help to keep their work afloat, and many of them recruited other French seminarians and clerics to join them in what was truly mission work. It was as if France — purified by its revolutionary agony — gave its brightest and best to the infant Church in the New World's first democracy. Perhaps some day the full story of these emigré priests will be set down for future generations. Some typical examples follow in the next several chapters.

# CHAPTER 7

## Our First Priest

### Stephen Badin

Stephen Theodore Badin, "the Apostle of Kentucky," was the first priest ordained in the United States. A small, slight man, he had the strength to endure the frontier life of Kentucky in his early years and the character not to spare himself in his later years in northern Indiana. He was a stern man of strict piety who had an uncompromising detestation for strong drink. He interpreted Church law narrowly. At the same time there was an attractiveness about him that drew people, and his sense of humor was greatly appreciated by those who knew him. A former archivist at the University of Notre Dame summed him up as "well educated, a writer of Latin verse, and an astute critic, whose proposals for the advancement of the Church brought success when followed and regret when neglected."

Father Badin was born in Orléans, France, on July 17, 1768, into a prosperous, middle-class family. He was educated in Orléans and was at college in Paris when he decided to become a priest. He entered the Sulpician seminary at Orléans; but when the bishop of that diocese took the constitutional oath to the revolutionary government, Badin decided that he could not serve under him. At precisely that time Father Benedict Joseph Flaget was visiting the seminary and challenging the students with missionary work in America. Young Badin decided to join him and with Flaget and John David arrived in Baltimore in March 1792; he became one of the first eight students in the new Sulpician seminary there. He was ordained by Bishop John Carroll on May 25, 1793, the first priest to receive ordination in the fledgling United States of America.

Bishop Carroll assigned Badin to the new state of Kentucky where there were about three hundred Catholic families, later appointing him vicar general for the state. (Kentucky had joined the Union just about a year before Badin's ordination.) Badin found the Catholics there to be poor and living in moral indifference. For three years he was the only priest in the state until he was joined by Fathers Michael Fournier and Anthony Salmon. He was tireless in his travels, making frequent visits north to Vincennes, Indiana, an old Catholic outpost which was at the time without a priest. He was the chief missioner in the western United States. He tried to persuade the Trappists to make a foundation in Kentucky; and although a delegate visited the area, Badin was disappointed when the Trappists decided otherwise. However, that same year (1793) a Belgian priest, Father Charles Nerinckx, did join him — and the Belgian was to become not only a valued co-worker but an outstanding recruiter of financial help and personnel. The following year Badin succeeded in getting the Dominicans under Father Edward Fenwick to settle in Kentucky and for a time thought of joining them.

Father Badin was a great writer, making frequent and detailed reports to Bishop Carroll. In one letter he complains: "It is afflicting, indeed, to see the Quakers, Presbyterians, Baptists, etc., have crept in and established their errors among tribes once taught the true religion by the Jesuits." To combat error he wrote *The Real Principles of Roman Catholics in Reference to God and the Country.* It was a clever work of apologetics which set down the basic tenets of the Catholic faith, followed by answers to the most common objections to Catholicism that were found on the frontier. He cultivated the editors of the few newspapers that existed and said that they gladly used material he gave them. While Vincennes was a center of Catholicism, most of the immigrants entering Indiana were Protestants, many of whom were attached to no church and were the object of attention by circuit-riding ministers.

Catholic settlers were coming into Kentucky, settling along the Ohio, White, and Wabash rivers. Their numbers increased so much that in 1808 the diocese of Bardstown was created and Benedict Flaget appointed bishop in 1810. (Incidentally, the see of Bardstown eventually was transferred to what is now the archdiocese of Louisville.) Flaget was well acquainted with the area and had served a pastorate in Vincennes. Although he and Badin were old acquaintances, it was not too long before the two men came into conflict. One point of disagreement was church lands which Badin held in his own name and refused to turn over to the bishop. Finally, Badin had enough and returned to France in 1819. He helped in French and Belgian parishes but could not forget the American frontier. While in France, Badin spent his time promoting the American missions and in raising funds and men to go to America. He was quite successful.

By 1828 the call to the wilderness grew too loud and Father Badin returned to America. A younger brother, Father Francis Vincent Badin, had followed his older sibling to America and was working with Father Gabriel Richard in Michigan, and the older Badin thought that would be a good place to begin anew. But first he visited friends in Kentucky, St. Louis, and New Orleans before going to Detroit. When he finally reached Michigan, Richard told him that the Potawatomi Indians were begging for a priest. This tribe had been converted years earlier by Jesuits; but after the Society of Jesus was suppressed, the Potawatomis fell away from the practice of their faith. The current chief, Pokagon — who had retained the Catholic religion — led a delegation from his tribe to ask for a priest. Richard was amazed that the Indians had retained the memory of common Catholic prayers, although none of them had ever seen a priest. He promised to try and help. The appearance of Father Stephen Badin was the answer to their prayers. Moreover, there were French settlers not far from the Indian village, remnants of the French who had gathered around Fort St. Joseph before its French soldiers were driven out.

When Father Badin heard the story, he agreed to go to the Potawatomis. Although sixty years of age and unfamiliar with the Indian tongue, Badin thought nothing of starting a new career on a new frontier. He took along an interpreter, Angelique Campau, an oldster like himself. Badin took up residence in the cabin of Chief Pokagon and with his interpreter went from cabin to cabin instructing the Indians, baptizing the children and those adults who were sufficiently instructed. He visited the French and half-breeds in the area along the St. Joseph River. He purchased land about two miles from the Indian village and opened a chapel. He instructed the Indians in agriculture and began to plan a school. He tried to get nuns and

more priests from Kentucky but was unsuccessful. He was continually on the move, administering to Catholics in southern Michigan, northern Indiana (including Fort Wayne, Logansport, and South Bend), and Chicago. A reporter for the *Catholic Miscellany* wrote in that paper, dated August 27, 1831: "During the hunting season the old gentleman visited Fort Wayne, at and near which he found about 100 Canadian Catholics. Having purchased a four-acre plot for the purpose of a church, they are now building one. In October he visited Chicago on the S.W. shore of Lake Michigan, where he found nearly 100 Canadians, and a tribe of sober, honest, peaceable and religious Indians, Kickapoos, who requested him to visit their village about 100 miles away. Father Badin resides on the south bend of the river St. Joseph, about equally distant from Fort Wayne and Chicago. There are perhaps upwards of eighty Canadians at this station." But the Indian part of Badin's work was coming to an end. The opening of the Erie Canal was bringing new settlers from New York and New England, and the Indians stood in their way. In what was to become a pattern across the width of America, the government moved the Indians westward. The Miami, Potawatomi, and other tribes were forced into a westward trek that caused many deaths and brought the tribes to near extinction. It was a part of history in which no American can take pride.

There was, however, plenty to do with the new arrivals, many of whom were Catholics. The Erie Canal was extended into Indiana; thus Fort Wayne and Wabash became the gateways to the West. This extension was to bring a host of Irish canal workers and German settlers. About this time the sixty-six-year-old Badin sent a report to then Bishop John Purcell. Dated September 23, 1834, the report read:

"I will not expatiate on the character of our Catholics. It is known that the lower class of the Irish, such as work on canals . . . is too fond of drinking, that there are very few of the devout sex, and few children among them. The Canadians are light headed, light footed, and very ignorant, having been without a pastor before I came to the backwoods, and being much intermixed with the Indians. The Germans are of much better disposition, as also the French from Lorraine and Alsace; but a priest familiar with the Dutch language is indeed wanted. — As to the Indians, the greater number of Christians are on the Michigan border. . . . The Poutouatamies of Mich. have sold all their lands and must migrate within two years. . . . The Indians are our best congre. — Town lots have been procured in five or six different places, viz. South Bend (one and a half miles from my establishment on St. Joseph River), Ft. Wayne, Huntington, Wabash and Logansport. . . . Prevailing sickness & mortality, the absence of a pastor & [the prevalence of] poverty have prevented the forwarding of Church affairs. . . . There should be two priests riding constantly every week along a line of 80 miles: They should be active, pious, learned and disinterested, courageous & mortified. . . . The character of our Cath. here has been so little respectable in general, that they rather confirm Protestant prejudices than are available to any conversion. O tempora, O mores!"

The report continues: "Our resource must lie in the education of youth. The introduction of Germans & German-French will offer also consolations to a resident pastor. Mr. Comparet estimates that the congre. in & about

116

Ft. Wayne must amount to 100 families. About three miles from that place a glebe-land [for a parish church] has been procured, but I have not yet paid nor can pay for it. — I'll close this information by adding that the Legisla. of Inda. has granted me a charter to establish St. Joseph Orphan Asylum. — Soli Deo honor & Gloria. Amen."

Thus the wilderness was disappearing as settlers came and took up farming. The old priest realized that a new day had come and that Catholics, if they were not to be left behind, had to be educated, hence his stress on schools. When he met Father Edward Sorin it was as if a prayer had been answered. The Holy Cross priest was interested in building not just a school but a college. Father Badin donated to Sorin the land on which the latter built the University of Notre Dame, and thus in a broad sense became a co-founder of that great institution. Times were changing. Other priests were coming into the area, and what Father Badin had covered alone would become many parishes and a half-dozen dioceses. A new time was coming, and the French who had preserved Catholicism on the American frontier from the time of the first fur trappers to almost the Civil War were to be replaced by priests of Irish and German ancestry. As the change began, Father Badin — aged and finally weary — went to visit his good friend Archbishop John Purcell in Cincinnati. There at the home of the archbishop the old French missionary died in the spring of 1853. Archbishop Purcell honored Badin's greatness by burying his spent body in the cathedral. In 1904 Stephen Theodore Badin's remains were transferred to the campus of the University of Notre Dame to lie in property he once owned but gave away because of his vision of the future.

# CHAPTER 8

## The Forgotten Bishop

### John Dubois

When this book was being prepared, I mentioned to a friend that I proposed to include Bishop John Dubois.

"Bishop who?" was the reply.

The response was not atypical. Few Catholic Americans — even those from his own diocese — can identify this man, who as much as anyone put his mark on the developing American Church. He trained several generations of leaders — archbishops, bishops, and outstanding priests and lay leaders. The ripples of his influence continue to this day.

John Dubois, unlike most emigrés, was a Parisian. He was born in the French capital on August 24, 1764. His mother was a widow, and one can only guess what education he might have received had he not won a scholarship to Louis-le-Grand College, where (similar to our own Boston Latin School) entrance was gained not by money or blood but by intellectual capacity. His brilliance was all the more remarkable, since he was two years younger than his classmates. Among his teachers and schoolmates were those destined to play decisive roles in the French Revolution, and one — Maximilien Robespierre — would step out of character and help him at a critical point in his life.

If John Dubois had remained at Louis-le-Grand after graduation, he would have undoubtedly become a teacher. But sometime during those restive years of France, God spoke to him and he answered. After graduating as a prize-winning scholar from his college, he entered St. Magloire Seminary for a career in the priesthood. He was ordained in 1787 with a dispensation because of his youth. The young abbé was assigned to the parish of St. Sulpice, a choice plum (probably earned because of his scholastic record) that served the elite of Paris. Among his parishioners were the Marquis de Lafayette and his wife. He was also assigned as chaplain to a large convent of Vincentian Sisters who conducted a home for the elderly and mentally ill. Those were heady times in Paris, with unrest and uncertainty for the future.

In early July of 1789, rioting broke out in Paris, and on July 14 the Bastille was stormed to release its political prisoners. The revolution had come, and it had the support of most priests who had lived with the indifference and injustice of royalty toward the commoners. Even at ritzy St. Sulpice, a "Te Deum" was sung and a Mass offered for those who had died in the Bastille attack.

But revolutions have a way of taking on a life of their own, and extremists frequently rise to the top. It was thus in Paris where radical, anticlerical elements — among them Abbé Dubois's old friend Robespierre — gained control. The radicals rammed through the Assembly the Civil Constitution of the Clergy, an act which made the Church wholly subservient to the state — with the state assigning bishops and pastors, seizing all religious assets, and removing all control from Rome. It became a moment of truth for the French clergy — either they took the oath to the new Constitution or they became pariahs. At Sunday Mass following the decree, the priests of St. Sulpice gathered in the sanctuary. They told the congregation that in conscience they could not take the oath demanded of them. Bedlam broke out and the police had to form a phalanx around the clergymen to get them safely into the sacristy.

The battle was joined, but there could only be one outcome. The revolutionists would not be constrained and priests who did not take the oath were forced out of their parishes to be replaced by those who were more pliant. Father Dubois was faced with a decision. He no longer had an ecclesiastical career in Paris and he anticipated rightly that darker days were to come. He had heard of the need for priests in the newly founded United States of America and he resolved to go there, but papers to get out of Paris and subsequent travel were needed. Bishop Simon Bruté, who became a confidant of Father Dubois in the United States, relates what happened: While pondering the problem of escape, Father Dubois one morning met his old schoolmate Robespierre, who had become a power in France. The two men had breakfast together, and despite being one of the main forces against the Church, the French anticleric supplied Father Dubois with papers that allowed him to escape to Le Havre and board a ship for Norfolk, Virginia, where the priest arrived in time to spend his twenty-seventh birthday. Lafayette had recommended James Monroe to him — they had served together in the American Revolution — and Father Dubois left for Richmond, where Monroe practiced law. Monroe, also a U.S. senator at the time, was imbued with the anti-Catholicism so prevalent in the former colonies. But what was a general dislike for Roman Catholicism disappeared in the particular case of the French priest. Monroe — future fifth president of the relatively new nation — welcomed the friend of a friend, and the two men developed a lasting respect for each other.

Under Monroe's sponsorship Father Dubois was well received in Richmond. Monroe had to leave for a congressional session, but Dubois's amiability and intelligence won new friends — among them Patrick Henry, who helped him learn English. (Not long after, the French priest became a citizen of the United States.) Catholicism had been banned when Virginia was a colony, so there were few Catholics in the state. Dubois covered the territory between Norfolk at one end and Charlottesville, Monroe's hometown, at the other. There were French exiles in the area, some from the home country and others from the Caribbean islands, whom he also served. To help support himself, the priest opened a school to teach French, Greek, Latin, arithmetic, and penmanship. News from France was dreadful; many of his friends had been put to death and his former parish church, St. Sulpice, had been desecrated. In 1794 Bishop John Carroll assigned Dubois to missionary work in Richmond as well as Norfolk. Eventually Dubois built the first Catholic church in Frederick, Maryland, with the help of a local Catholic, Roger Brooke Taney — who was to become attorney general of the United States and the first Catholic chief justice of the Supreme Court, and who would be remembered in history for the Dred Scott Case. With Frederick as his base, Dubois rode the circuit for the next ten years caring for scattered Catholics wherever he could find them.

It is a commentary on the times and the needs that a man of Father Dubois's learning and talent should be an itinerant missioner. It is also a tribute to his own humility and dedication that he should undertake the difficult life

121

of a traveling priest, not only willingly but gladly. One of the places he liked to visit was Emmitsburg, a small village northwest of Baltimore that was a center for Catholics. Nearby was Elder Station; the Elders were old-line Catholics, descending from the earliest Catholic settlers in Maryland. The Elders had a large chapel on their farm where he would say Mass.

The Elders gave Dubois a piece of land to build a church for the Emmitsburg region; but before he began construction, he discovered another site on a hillside overlooking the valley. It had a spring and an abundance of firewood. He bought the property in 1805, invited Catholics and Protestants to help clear it in a day, at the end of which he gave all who helped an ox roast. He named his church St. Mary's and bought land surrounding it for future use. He made the new parish his center and it became a stopover for Sulpicians traveling between a minor seminary they had in Pennsylvania, near Gettysburg, and their Baltimore major seminary. Dubois had remained close to the Sulpicians since arriving in Maryland. He stayed at St. Mary's Seminary whenever he went to Baltimore, made his annual retreat there, and had applied for admission into the society (which Paris had not yet granted). When the rector of St. Mary's stayed with him one night, the Sulpician suggested that the Emmitsburg property would be ideal for the minor seminary. Dubois agreed.

In 1807 Father Dubois was admitted to the Sulpicians. The first charge given him as a new member was to build a preparatory seminary. He dug out a level area on the mountainside and erected two log buildings. In 1809 the first eighteen students arrived and Mount St. Mary's

Seminary was underway. That year also saw another responsibility fall to Dubois through the "kindness" of the Baltimore rector. Elizabeth Seton, a widowed convert (whose full story is narrated in Chapter 13), had gone to Baltimore with her five children to open a school there at the suggestion of Bishop Carroll, who had placed her under the care of the rector, Father Louis William Dubourg. Mother Seton had gathered a few women around her to help, and there was talk of starting a religious community. Dubourg, who was a great man for delegation, concluded that Emmitsburg would be an ideal place for Mother Seton, and Dubois was exactly the man to get her started; so Dubourg packed her, her children, her assistants, and their belongings into some wagons and sent them off on the fifty miles to Emmitsburg. Of course, nothing was ready and Dubois had to move out of his own small house to give shelter to the women and children. A small stone house on the Elder farm was then fixed up for them while a permanent shelter was built. Dubois — in mulling over the fact that Mrs. Seton's children included two boys who had to be educated — decided that his seminary would be a college as well.

I suppose an ordinary man might have thrown up his hands and walked away from all the responsibilities suddenly thrown at him, but Father Dubois was far from ordinary. He accepted the task of feeding, clothing, and sheltering the women. He discussed with Mrs. Seton her plans — and from his experience with the nuns in Paris where he had been chaplain, he drew up a constitution and rules. He sat at his table and drew plans for their first convent: two stories, topped by attic rooms, that would be known as the White House. He made plans for his own future college, fashioning the plans after those of Louis-le-Grand College. It was no easy time for the Father on the Mountain, as Dubois was called. He had fifty people to care for, and where there are people there are people-related problems. He had problems with the weather, with a faulty building, with lack of funds. Moreover, Father Dubourg was pushing Mother Seton to place her new community under the Daughters of Charity in France, while he, Father Dubois, was for an independent American community. Dubois won out when Bishop Carroll appointed him superior of the new community.

Relief came to the overburdened Mountain priest in the fall of 1812 when Simon Bruté (whose story will be told in detail in the next chapter) came as his assistant. Father Bruté had arrived in America two years earlier from France. He had been assigned to the Baltimore seminary as a teacher, but his many talents and his rapport with the Sisters made him very desirable for Emmitsburg. Father Dubois had sought to obtain the young priest through the Sulpician superior and Bishop Carroll. It took two years of pleas and entreaties for the change to be made. Bruté taught classes, acted as chaplain for the Sisters, and served in any capacity assigned him. The respite gave Dubois the chance to get his head above water. He expanded his college, accepting any boy who wanted an education — and if the boys who were accepted could not pay, Dubois found employment for them at the college. One of these, John Hughes — who was destined to be Dubois's coadjutor bishop — was hired as a gardener in lieu of tuition. Other students included John Purcell (who was to become the first archbishop of Cincinnati) and John McCloskey (who was to become the first cardinal in the United States).

Then troubles began. Bruté — unwillingly — was called back to Baltimore as president of St. Mary's Seminary. He besieged Paris with letters about why he should go back to Mount St. Mary's. When the only other priest at the Mount — a bedridden Father Charles Duhamel — died, Father Bruté "unassigned" himself from Baltimore and hurried back to the Mount. Father Dubois did not disapprove of the disobedience, and this angered the Baltimore Sulpicians who informed Paris that the Mount should be shut down as financially unsound. The new archbishop of Baltimore, Ambrose Maréchal, was a Sulpician. He sided with the Baltimore Sulpicians and observed: "Mr. Dubois does not have the faintest idea of the spirit of St. Sulpice" and added, "nor does Mr. Bruté." However, the two men under attack had the ear of the superior general, largely through letters sent by Father Bruté. Next the Baltimore Sulpicians argued that Father Dubois was giving too much time to Mother Seton's group, that it was the work of the society to train priests, not Sisters. The flow of letters and the battle ended when France decided that Mount St. Mary's would be transferred from the jurisdiction of Baltimore and made the full responsibility of Dubois. Since nothing was said about the Sisters, he continued as their superior. It was now Dubois's responsibility to get his own helpers and he solved this problem by keeping the graduates of the preparatory seminary to teach, thus by force beginning a major seminary, which was to train a steady line of priests.

In 1821, shortly after the new year, Mother Seton died. Her community had grown, and Father Dubois — as superior — had sent her Sisters to open orphanages and schools in Philadelphia and New York. He next negotiated work for them in Baltimore: caring for the poor, teaching catechism, and working in an infirmary. The plans he had drawn up for his college, a three-story building that was reminiscent of his Paris school, were pulled out and construction was begun.

The new seminary was almost completed, with furniture and some students moved in, when fire broke out in the attic on a Sunday night in 1824. In a short time the whole building was ablaze. The students worked heroically, passing buckets of water; but the best they could do was save the old building next to it. The new seminary was a total loss. The *Catholic Miscellany* reported that "the fire has been communicated by some fiend in human form." The cause was a mystery. The students met and — after passing a resolution of sympathy and support for Father Dubois "for his past affectionate and tender regard for our welfare" — announced a two-hundred-dollar reward "for the conviction of the wretch, who has thus endeavoured to blast the most flattering prospects of this useful establishment." It was suspected that a workman had set the blaze to ensure additional employment, but nothing was ever proved and the reward went unclaimed. The *Catholic Miscellany* made an appeal for funds. Dubois was heartened by the support of his students as well as that of alumni and friends. He accepted the tragedy as God's will, saying that he had probably made a mistake anyway in locating the building on the upper terrace. He set about rebuilding in a different location.

The Baltimore Sulpicians took the occasion to once again insist that the Emmitsburg institution be reduced to a minor seminary; they wanted no competition with their Baltimore schools. Dubois and Bruté talked over the order. They discussed trying to find a bishop to take over the seminary or even starting a new religious order that would ensure the seminary's continuance. Dubois wrote to Archbishop Maréchal of the "sad experience which I have had from the moment of my union with a foreign society." But when the students returned from their summer vacations with the money they had raised begging for the new college-seminary, his spirits were rejuvenated. Both he and Bruté told the Sulpicians they would not retreat from their position. The superior in Paris sent word that they were expelled from the Sulpicians. History shows that it was the Sulpicians' loss.

If Mount St. Mary's was to continue, its president was not. Although neither man had any inkling of it, Father Bruté would have to carry on alone. In 1826 John Connolly — the second bishop of New York — died. The two leading candidates for the vacant see were Benedict Fenwick and John Power. In the consultation made by Propaganda for the vacant post those two names headed the *terna*, or list of three nominees. The third choice of many was John Dubois. Not too long before he died, Bishop Connolly had written to Propaganda concerning the importance of having someone from Ireland in the New York post because the "Catholic population consists chiefly of Irishmen; they build the churches and expect priests to understand them." There were many others who felt the same way. At the same time Archbishop Maréchal had complained to Propaganda that four out of five Irish priests who came to America were failures.

Father Power, who had come from Ireland in 1818, badly wanted the job. He gained the support of his Irish colleague John England, first bishop of Charleston, and solicited support in New York. He sent testimonials to Propaganda, along with petitions he had instigated among priests, church trustees, and others. It was a mistake on his part because the Holy See does not like to be pressured, particularly in the appointment of bishops.

At the time all of this was going on, the Boston see also became vacant. Some of the French bishops wrote to Propaganda to suggest that New York and Boston be combined because there were so few Catholics in either diocese. Most of them favored Fenwick for either see because he was a native American, without allegiance to "foreign parties." Rome first filled the Boston post, naming Fenwick. Power resumed his campaign for New York in the belief that he no longer had competition. It was another mistake. Rome considered the names it had, and in comparing what Power had done in New York — nothing of permanence — and what Dubois had accomplished, the scales were definitely weighted. On April 30, 1826, the pope named John Dubois bishop of New York.

The appointment had various reactions. Those at Mount St. Mary's were upset at losing their president and fearful of a future without him. Archbishop Maréchal even protested to Propaganda in this vein. The Irish of New York were up in arms. "The French junta of Baltimore had seized the fruits of Irish labor. Will Irishmen permit it?" thundered one newspaper. To his discredit Father Power not only did nothing to still the tempest but subtly fired it. A member of the Sisters of Charity in New York wrote Dubois, "I fear so much if you do come to this place you will find much less happiness than you may now imagine awaits you." She was prophetic. Father Dubois himself, who could have refused the post, hesitated. He was no longer young, he was wrapped up in what he thought was his life's work, and he sensed the problems that were probably awaiting him. He debated the matter and in the end decided that the action of the pope represented the will of God. He accepted and began winding up his affairs at the Mount, leaving it in the hands of Father Simon Bruté.

Bishop Dubois was consecrated October 29, 1826, in the Baltimore cathedral by Archbishop Maréchal (who was to die in January of 1828). Dubois's students came down from Emmitsburg for the occasion. An old friend, Charles Carroll of Carrollton (one of the signers of the Declaration of Independence), made him the gift of an episcopal cross and ring. To help appease his New York critics, the new bishop put the shamrock on his episcopal coat of arms. It was a happy occasion, giving little evidence of the dark night of the soul which lay ahead.

Bishop Dubois sailed for New York on the *Commodore Perry*. The *Catholic Miscellany* reported his arrival in New York but devoted most of its article to the praise of Father Power — which was not unexpected, as the *Miscellany* editor, Bishop John England, had been one of Power's backers. In the article praising Power, England had this to say about Dubois's ascendancy to the diocese of New York: "Though we are ready to bow with respect to whatever appointment Rome may make to the see of New-York, yet we know of no Clergyman on the American Mission more worthy of this Bishoprick or more likely to advance the best interests of Religion in that large and important diocese." If the third bishop of New York had a reaction to this dig at him, he did not show it.

Bishop Dubois ignored the controversy, asking only

that he be judged by his acts. One of his first duties was the ordination of one of his Mountain boys, Luke Berry. Father Berry was to serve in New York and Utica, and die an early death in the latter post. Next, he wrote a pastoral letter offering an olive branch to those who opposed him. He spoke of his work in Maryland. He praised Bishop Connolly and Father Power, saying that the latter had done "all but impossibilities." As for his own appointment: "So far from considering it a reward we view it as the last sacrifice we can make to duty and religion." Father Thomas Levins, a cohort of Father Power, would not even print the pastoral in his newspaper. These two priests would not be appeased and used their influence among parish trustees to snipe at the bishop. Not everyone, however, opposed Dubois. Among the new bishop's chief supporters, for instance, was Pierre Toussaint, an ex-slave who had prospered in freedom and was a man of great spiritual strength.

John Dubois found relief from clerical politics in visiting his vast diocese. On these trips he could seek out lost Catholics and fulfill the duties of a priest — baptizing, hearing confessions, witnessing marriages. He found that there were far more Catholics than anyone had thought: "Seven hundred where I understand there were but fifty or sixty, eleven hundred where I was told to look for two hundred." The old missioner had not lost his touch. His diocese included Indian reservations in upstate New York, most with many lost Catholics, who retained old ways taught them by Jesuit missioners. On the reservations, he felt at home for the first time since arriving in New York. By 1834 he had nineteen parishes: five in New York; one in Brooklyn; one in the Hudson Valley; ten across the center of the state from Albany to Buffalo; and two in New Jersey (Newark and Trenton). He noted the need for schools and wanted to start them but was thwarted by trustees who would not authorize the money. A group of Irish Christian Brothers came to open both a free school and one charging tuition, but his joy was turned to sadness when the group withdrew because the trustees wanted not only title to any property they might obtain but also the decision on accepting or rejecting Brothers. Perhaps Bishop Dubois — now getting on in years — would have done better to take on the trustees directly; but he was a gentle person and a man of peace who expected others to be like him. He had another dream, that of a seminary. Several times he had money for the project, only to have to use it for more urgent needs of a church in Albany and then one in New Jersey. In 1832 he had enough money saved and bought a farm at Nyack on the Hudson River. Once again he drew plans and undertook construction. Father John Power attacked the project, as could be expected.

However, Power, the pastor of St. Peter's on Barclay Street, was clever. He never took the bishop head-on but attacked him behind his back and through others. He was constantly writing letters to his friends in the United States and in Rome. He instigated others to more direct action, one of them being Father Levins. Again Bishop Dubois — who knew what was going on — refrained, out of mildness. He was a pastor, not a punisher. He had to take action, however, when Father Levins went too far. When the priest refused to take a sick call, the pastor in Bishop Dubois acted. He told Levins that he must learn his duty and that if he refused another sick call, he was suspended *ipso facto*. Levins, calling the bishop "imperious," wrote, "If you wish for war, at once declare it. I am ready." He refused to cover sick calls which came to St. Patrick's. It was a challenge the bishop could not ignore. He withdrew Father Levins's faculties and interdicted him "from all pastoral functions in this diocese." From then on Levins was really brutal in his attacks against Dubois.

Another trial the bishop had was the rise of anti-Catholicism under the guise of Native Americanism. Attacks in the press against the Church, particularly the Sisterhood, were virulent. The Protestant press mounted harsh slanders; but even the more restrained *New York Herald* — which frequently attacked Bishop Dubois — ranted against French and Italian control of the Church and praised the Irish boards of trustees which "have been aiming for years to establish the independence of their Church against the powers of Rome." The Protestants imported Maria Monk, whose *Awful Disclosures* of what she said went on in convents had become a best seller, and she became the toast of Protestant society. The bubble burst, however, when the *Herald* reported that "the enchanting Miss Maria Monk is again *enceinte*" and said that the father-to-be was a Presbyterian parson, adding the names of five reverends she had been in company with.

While the *Herald* would attack both Catholics and Protestants, the heavy guns were against Catholics. When a mob in Boston burned down an Ursuline convent, Protestant papers applauded the action. Locally, Protestant papers — such as the *Intelligencer* and the *Vindicator* — warned about the "monastery" (actually the seminary) that Bishop Dubois had built in Nyack. The *Intelligencer*

133

suggested that fire was a purifier. It should not have been surprising, then, when the Nyack seminary was burned to the ground in 1834. Like the Mount St. Mary's fire ten years earlier, nothing could be proved. The bishop observed that in the present life he was being tried by fire and hoped that it would not be true in the next. Attacks against his churches continued.

As he approached the fiftieth anniversary of his priesthood, Bishop Dubois knew that the sands of his life were running out. He proposed to Rome and his fellow bishops that an assistant be appointed for New York. The American bishops endorsed the idea. When he celebrated his anniversary in September 1837, five thousand people came to St. Patrick's to rejoice with him. He was particularly pleased that thirty-four priests were present, a remarkable number considering the difficulties of travel in that era. What made him happy was that most of them were priests he had trained on the Mountain.

News arrived that Rome had approved a coadjutor, John Hughes of Philadelphia, and what was particularly gratifying to the old bishop was that Hughes was a Mountain boy who had worked his way through the seminary. In early January of 1838 Bishop Dubois consecrated John Hughes as a bishop and his assistant. It is possible that the team of "father and son" might have worked out; but within a month Bishop Dubois had his first stroke, to be quickly followed by another that was even more serious.

The old man had never known ill health and had always been responsible for his own actions. Now he was incapacitated and partly paralyzed. It was Bishop Hughes who had to take over the missionary journeys and the burdens of the diocese. He told Bishop John Purcell that there were many problems in the diocese because Bishop Dubois ruled with his heart and not his head, and that the problems were not being solved because the bishop would not delegate power. He wrote to Archbishop Samuel Eccleston of Baltimore that the bishop was too feeble but would not admit it. When Bishop Dubois had another stroke early in 1839, Bishop Hughes went directly to Propaganda, stating the ailing bishop's condition and adding that things were at a standstill because he himself had no authority.

Rome acted. Archbishop Eccleston received an order from Propaganda to relieve Bishop Dubois of jurisdiction over his diocese. As an act of kindness the archbishop decided that he would carry the order himself rather than give it to the impersonal mails. Bishop Purcell happened to be in the city at the time and he offered to accompany the archbishop, since his old master was fond of him. But there was no way to really soften the blow. "What have I done?" asked Dubois. "How can Rome do this to me? I will not give up." Purcell persuaded his "father" that it was for the good of the Church, and to this the old bishop finally yielded.

The same scene has been played out many times. Hughes, of course, was correct; but he was a cold person who was not capable of showing emotion and thus speaking to the heart of the old man. Hughes simplified his new authority by ignoring the old bishop. Dubois, for his part, thought of Hughes as a youth he had trained, inexperienced and unwilling to use the expertise of years. Bishop John Dubois made one last visit to the Mount, staying in Mother Seton's old room. The Sisters who knew him were saddened to see this once active man tottering about and stumbling over his thoughts. It was suggested that he spend his last days there, but he insisted that he had to return to his work in New York. Within six months after returning to New York he was dead. The date was December 20, 1842.

Bishop Dubois did not have a big funeral. Bishop Francis Kenrick was to come to New York to preach but could not make it. Bishop 'Hughes took Kenrick's place and, as the *Herald* noted, "Of the deceased, Bishop Hughes spoke little." Bishop Dubois was buried beneath Mulberry Street, in front of the cathedral. Hughes did not bother to have the old bishop's grave marked, and people began forgetting Dubois. The times were becoming turbulent and Hughes would have his own problems. Within years, even the memory of Dubois's grave was lost. One hundred and thirty-five years later an archdiocesan official wondered where New York's third bishop was buried. Historians began a search and in time the tomb was found. Now it is covered with a white slab, and there is a plaque on Old St. Patrick's in memory of the great contribution Bishop John Dubois made to the developing Church of America.

# CHAPTER 9

## *Bishop on Horseback*

### *Simon Bruté*

Of all the emigrés who came to the United States, Simon Bruté was the most remarkable. (His full name was Simon William Gabriel Bruté de Rémur.) He was not only a priest and bishop but was also a graduate physician, an artist, an architect, a skilled writer, and one who seemed to be able to do anything to which he put his hand. "You were born to live in opulence," his mother frequently said to him as a child. Instead, he chose to live the hard life of the American frontier.

Simon Bruté was born on March 20, 1779, in Rennes, capital of Brittany (a province of France), where his father was superintendent of the royal finances. His mother was a strong-willed woman of deep faith who was to hide priests during the French Revolution. The family lived in the Palace of Parliament. "My earliest recollections," Bruté wrote, "are connected with the entertainment given by my father, at his residence in the city and at his country house. . . . I remember seeing no less than five of our bishops at his table at one time." However, when Simon was one month short of his seventh birthday, his father died as a result of a fall from a horse. His mother, who must have been a remarkable woman in her own right, took over the management of her husband's affairs. The young Simon made his first Holy Communion in 1791, the last year of religious freedom in France.

Although Bruté was only a child when the French Revolution began, his journals record many happenings of those days and he sometimes accompanied those recollections with sketches. One of the latter shows a revolutionary tribunal trying a priest and several nuns, and he indicates in his journal that the usual verdict was death or banishment to French Guiana. He records the heroic deaths of some of his teachers and friends. He also tells how he — although only a boy — made friends with prison guards so that he could smuggle letters and the Blessed Sacrament to those awaiting the guillotine. His mother had him work in her printing office during this period so that he would not be enlisted into a children's regiment whose members were allowed to condemn some victims and then execute them by shooting. As a result of this experience, he recalled, "I became a very good compositor." His Catholic school had, of course, been closed and — during the height of the terror — he was educated privately. When the excesses began to abate, he attended public school, where he excelled. He had a prodigious memory, and as one who knew him in later life remarked, "Whatever he once read, he remembered." This was proven by his ease in quoting long passages from French and Latin classical writers.

When he was seventeen, Bruté began the study of medicine in Rennes and then moved on to Paris where he found his professors contemptuous of his Catholic faith. He did not hesitate to oppose their gibes and defend his beliefs. He encouraged many of his classmates to do the same thing. In 1803 he graduated from medical school with the highest honors and at the top of his class. He received an appointment as a state physician and, to the surprise of all, refused it by entering the reopened seminary of St. Sulpice to prepare for the priesthood.

Napoleon Bonaparte had succeeded the revolutionary tribunals and was attempting to restore order in France. Seminaries which had been closed for a decade were allowed to reopen and France was in great need of priests, since the clergy had been decimated by murders, banishment, or voluntary exile. In the seminary, Bruté repeated his scholastic triumphs, filling notebooks that would be useful to him. He was particularly skilled in apologetics. As he approached ordination, he began considering what he wanted to do with his priesthood. With his talent and skill he could expect to rise to high honors in the French Church, yet he was not interested in worldly rewards. His notes reveal that he was thinking of India where all of what he had learned could be put to use in the salvation of souls.

Simon Bruté was ordained in 1808. Both the bishop of Nantes and the bishop of Rennes bid for his services and he was also offered a post as assistant chaplain to the emperor Napoleon. He accepted the offer of the bishop of Rennes to be a professor of theology in his diocesan seminary, although he declined an appointment to be also a canon in the Rennes cathedral. He was still thinking of India when Father Benedict Flaget paid a visit to his home country in 1810. Father Flaget was one of the band of Sulpician emigrés who had gone to the fledgling United States when the Revolution closed their work in France. For some years he had been working under primitive conditions in Kentucky. His purpose in returning to France was to try to escape a new responsibility that had been thrust upon him. Bishop John Carroll had asked Rome to split his huge diocese, which embraced the entire United States. Rome had agreed and one of the four new dioceses to be erected was Bardstown, with Father Flaget selected as its first bishop, an honor he would have preferred to avoid.

In Paris the Sulpician superior general persuaded Father Flaget to accept. Once that decision was made, Flaget took advantage of the trip home to visit relatives and seek support — in both finances and vocations — for the American missions. One of those who heard Flaget's message was the young seminary professor of Rennes. He quickly decided that God was calling him to America and not India. Thus when Flaget sailed from Bordeaux for Baltimore in mid-1810, Bruté was with him. The young French priest arrived in Baltimore on August 10 and was assigned to begin teaching philosophy at St. Mary's Seminary that fall. He was sent out to a mission parish for experience and to learn English. A letter relates: ". . . I serve with Father Monaly, at St. Joseph's. . . . I am trying to learn practically my English. I have said Mass and preached, bad preaching as it may be, in six different places. This must force this dreadful English into my backward head or I must renounce forever to know it."

Father Bruté's next assignment was to Mount St. Mary's in Emmitsburg. The town was a mission station before the American Revolution and was situated in the mountains on the Pennsylvania-Maryland border. Catholics had settled in the area and were being served by the Sulpicians, who had opened a school and a preparatory seminary. Father John Dubois, a talented and energetic man, was in charge. The school had become a college, popular with Catholic parents, and Dubois needed help.

140

Bruté was the answer. Archbishop James Roosevelt Bayley — a nephew of St. Elizabeth Seton — who wrote the first life of Bishop Bruté, says of him: "Father Bruté could never have hoped to do as much good among the inhabitants of India and China, by the exertion of the highest apostolic zeal, as he was permitted to do in this country. It is no disparagement of those holy and eminent men who have adorned the annals of the Catholic Church in America — of a Carroll, a Cheverus, a Dubois, and a Flaget — to say that no one has ever exerted a more beneficial influence in favor of the Catholic religion than Bishop Bruté."

Father Bruté's work consisted of teaching and handling affairs at the college and caring for the needs of Catholics in the area. He used another skill he had — cartography — to draw a map showing the roads, topography, and the location of the home of every Catholic family within a twenty-mile radius of the college. He rose at 4:30 in the morning and went until ten at night. When he was not teaching he traveled extensively, visiting Catholic families. An entry in his journal, in his sometimes imperfect English, tells us: "I remember to have spoken to 62 persons, more probably, in regards to matters connected with their religion and their duty. . . . Three persons were warned about their Easter duty; several spoken to for circulating evil reports; others warned against attending a camp meeting to begin next week." He used every minute, so as not to waste time, even in his travels; another entry about a journey to Baltimore points out: "In going I read 388 pages in D'Anguetil's *History of France*, the reigns of Louis XII and Francis I; 14 pages of Cicero's *De Officiis*, 3 chapters in the New Testament; my office;

recited the Chaplet three times. On my journey back, the wind blew so hard, that I could only read a Pamphlet of 25 pages (Documents of the Bishop of Philadelphia) and my office."

When he became superior of the Emmitsburg foundation, his schedule greatly increased. He became the director and confidant of Mother Elizabeth Seton, who had located the motherhouse of her Sisters of Charity near the college. He helped Mother Seton meet the problems of both her family and young community. He tended her in her final illness and blessed her dead body, which he accompanied to the grave. Because of his knowledge and common sense he was often called upon for advice by bishops and he was an important resource for ecclesiastical councils. An eager apologist, he would allow no attack on his Roman Catholic faith to go unanswered, and his letters appeared in newspapers and magazines. He also carried on a prolific correspondence, not only with superiors and friends in France, but throughout the states. He and Judge William Gaston, a prominent Catholic of North Carolina, sent letters back and forth, as he did with Charles Carroll of Carrollton, the Declaration of Independence signer.

There are many stories of the impoverished around Emmitsburg and needy students receiving Simon Bruté's charity. Bruté went out on distant sick calls at any hour and in any weather. One of his greatest joys was to bring Communion to those sick at home. His journal is full of such examples of his charity: "8 o'C at Mrs. McCormick's; her lively marks of faith and joy; heard her confession; arranged the table; called the people; the young convert and her little one; her husband preparing for his First Communion; administered the Blessed Sacrament to Mrs. McC; spoke of Martha and Mary and Lazarus and Zacheus, old friends of our Lord on earth. . . . On our way to Emmitsburg, recited the Miserere, our Father, Hail Mary; hymn, 'Jesus lover of my Soul.' " When a cholera epidemic broke out in Baltimore, he hastened there to tend the sick. He became ill himself and went back to the Mount to recover; as soon as he was well again, he returned to the Baltimore hospitals until the disease had run its course.

In 1833 the Second Provincial Council of Baltimore requested the Holy See to establish a new diocese, centered at Vincennes, Indiana. The council recommended that Father Simon Bruté be appointed its bishop. When Bruté heard the news, in typical fashion, he listed on a sheet of paper all the reasons why he should accept and why he should decline; naturally the latter received the most attention from him. However, the archbishop of Baltimore informed him that the matter was settled, so Bruté put away his list and drew a map of his mission territory which embraced all of Indiana and the eastern half of Illinois. He noted that Vincennes was the thirteenth diocese to be erected in the United States. He made his farewells at the Mount (the Sisters of Charity presented him with two hundred dollars), went to Bardstown to make his retreat, and then continued to St. Louis where on October 28, 1834, he was consecrated by his old friend Bishop Benedict Flaget. The first bishop of Vincennes was fifty-five years old, and if he wondered about age being a factor in his new work, he does not mention it in any of his writings. Bishop Flaget accompanied the new bishop back to Vincennes so that he could be properly installed.

Bishop Bruté was both pastor of Vincennes diocese and of Vincennes parish. His nearest priest was about thirty miles distant; another priest labored in the Fort Wayne area, some two hundred miles northeast as the crow flies. The bishop of St. Louis had loaned him a priest for a year and he assigned him to Chicago, where some people were settling among the Indians. He brought Sisters from Kentucky to open a school in Vincennes. He also brought his large library from Emmitsburg, an incredible feat in itself. He drew up plans for a cathedral, which he named after St. Francis Xavier, of whom he had some precious relics. Although he was often on the road, he kept up his apologetic articles, adopting a new signature, "Vincennes"; he also wrote for the Catholic paper in Cincinnati, carried on an extensive correspondence (he had to raise funds to keep his diocese going), and wrote faithfully in his journal.

Bishop Bruté set out on an inspection of his vast territory, traveling by horseback, seeking out Catholics, staying wherever he could find someone to give him shelter. He visited Indian camps and discovered that many of them were already Catholics. He went to St. Mary of the Lake, near South Bend, to see a piece of property — six hundred twenty-five acres — that Father Stephen Badin had bought for a mission house and which had been transferred to the new diocese. He noted that it is "a most desirable spot, and one day soon I hope to . . . [see it] occupied by some prosperous institution." These trips which would occupy him for much of the rest of his life were arduous for a young man and particularly difficult for an aging bishop. But always there were souls to be found, lost Catholics to be restored to the Church, bap-

tisms long delayed, marriages to be blessed, confessions heard.

Bishop Bruté had a great fondness for the Ottawa Indians of Indiana, whom he found equal to "the best instructed Christians of more favored countries." He was impressed by their deep faith and trust, and moved by their generosity, although they had little to give. The Indians called him the chief of the Blackrobes, subject only to the chief of all Christians (the pope). Although they gave him their best, it was never much. In describing a typical visit he wrote: "We slept on the benches of the chapel, and some of the straw from the floor, wrapped up in our great coats after the manner of the good father. Our food was boiled corn, fish, venison, and wild turkey, minced together in one dish, and some cranberries broken and mixed with sugar which they get from trees. Our drink was water." This was somewhat different from the opulence which his widowed mother had envisioned for him.

But it was consoling work and not once in his journal does the bishop make a complaint. He established a seminary, an academy, a free school, and an orphan asylum. He made a trip to France and recruited twenty priests and seminarians. He opened new parishes, writing twice a month to each of his priests. His journals became a contemporary history of the Church in the Midwest. He was able to rise above difficulties and found ways to carry out his plans. Above all, as so many testified, he was a father to his priests and a good pastor to his people.

Traveling for weeks on horseback can wear down even the hardiest, and eventually age and debilitating disease ended Bishop Bruté's journeys. He wrote letters to his priests encouraging them in his stead. As his strength diminished, his prayerfulness increased, as if knowingly he was preparing himself for that one final, great journey. The day came when he could no longer walk or stand, so he would sit at his desk and write letters; even up to six hours before his death, he was still writing, this time to two people who had abandoned the faith. He predicted the moment of his death, and told friends simply, "I am going home." The end came on June 26, 1839. He was buried under the sanctuary of the cathedral he had built, now a basilica, where Catholics and Protestants came to bid him farewell.

# CHAPTER 10

## *The Mountain Man*

### *Joseph Machebeuf*

It is unfortunate that too few Catholics are familiar with the name of Joseph P. Machebeuf. This great missioner was a pioneer priest in Ohio, New Mexico, and Colorado. For many years he lived in the shadow of Archbishop John Lamy, whose career in Santa Fe was immortalized by Willa Cather in her novel *Death Comes for the Archbishop*. Machebeuf plays an important role also in that book, but again it is subordinate to Lamy's. Yet much for which Lamy is credited, Machebeuf accomplished. Machebeuf left behind him an abundance of correspondence, mainly to his family, from which can be reconstructed the life of a pioneer priest in a developing America.

Joseph P. Machebeuf was born on August 11, 1812, at Riom, in Auvergne, France. He was baptized Projectus Joseph after his grandfather and in honor of St. Projectus, a former bishop of Auvergne. Later when he came to America, because his first name was strange to American ears, he switched the two names and was known thereafter as Joseph P. Machebeuf. His first education was with the Christian Brothers, and from them he passed on to a college at Riom which had been seized in the French Revolution from the religious order that ran it and was still in the hands of the anticlericals. For a time he thought of a military career, but in 1831 he entered the Sulpician seminary in Montferrand. It was here he began writing his long letters home, a practice he was to continue all his life. He was ordained in 1836 and assigned to a parish near Clermont, but he was uncertain if this was the course God meant for him. While in the seminary, he had heard a Vincentian priest speak on the American missions and the thought had stayed with him, not as a resolution but as a growing seed.

The seed became a resolution when Bishop Benedict Flaget, a missioner in America for forty-three years, visited Auvergne and spoke about his work. Among those who heard him was young Father Machebeuf. Bishop Flaget's talk brought the seed to bloom and during a retreat that year Machebeuf made the decision to go to the American missions. He confided his resolution to a friend from seminary days — another young priest, whose name was John Lamy — and discovered his friend had the same idea. Father Machebeuf did not want to face his father, who he expected would have strong objections; so before sunrise on May 21, 1839, he and Father Lamy stole quietly out of town and boarded the stage to Paris. There they went to the Paris Foreign Mission Society seminary on the Rue de Bac where Machebeuf wrote a long letter to his father, explaining his abrupt departure and his decision to answer what he believed was God's call.

At the Paris seminary, the young priests met their new bishop, John Purcell of Cincinnati, who was also in France seeking recruits and money. When Bishop Purcell heard the story of the secret departure, he in turn wrote to the senior Machebeuf and told what France had contributed to the American Church. He concluded his letter: "Adieu, good father. I bid you farewell for your dear son, who is now not only yours but mine also, that is, of two fathers instead of one. I shall love him for you; he will pray for you on earth, and in heaven by the numerous souls whom God proposes to save through ... [your son's] ministry." The two letters accomplished their purpose and Monsieur Machebeuf was reconciled to the loss of his son.

The group that boarded the *Sylvie de Grasse* at Le Havre on July 9, 1839, included Bishop Purcell, Bishop Flaget (and his vicar general), five priest volunteers, and a number of Sisters. Father Machebeuf wrote his father about the journey. There were sixty passengers in his section of the ship, mostly Protestants (a new experience for him). In steerage were nearly two hundred Germans (mostly peasants), a few Catholics, and forty Jews. "This is but a sample," he wrote, "of the incredible number of immigrants arriving in the United States from all parts. Judge for yourself, then, if priests are not necessary, both to sustain the faith of Catholics and bring back the heretics." He describes the difficult conditions of the immigrants, all lodged in one room where they ate, slept, and spent the day. They had to bring their own food and "the Captain furnishes them only with wood and water." As for the priests, "we are treated too well for missioners." He relates that neither he nor Bishop Flaget became seasick, although Bishop Purcell was sick for three days and Father Lamy for three weeks. The travelers reached New York on August 21 and went the rest of the way by canal and stagecoach, reaching Cincinnati the second week of September.

Father Machebeuf was assigned almost immediately to Tiffin, Ohio, where he learned that an American missioner was a man on the go. In his letters home he revealed that his parish embraced nine counties, "each county as large as a department in France." Telling in a letter how the priests traveled by buggy, he observed: "Today, after a journey of thirty or forty miles I am less tired than I would be in France after a couple of leagues." He discovered that while it was the custom in France for priests to wear a cassock all the time, it was not the case in America. "On the streets, or when we go to the missions, we wear a frock coat, waistcoat and trousers, with a black cravat, and everyone recognizes us as Catholic priests." His only complaint — and it was a minor one — was the lack of companionship. "You ask me if I see my companions often? I must answer like the Gascon — I see them every time I find an occasion but I am still on the lookout for the first occasion. Father Lamy is the nearest one to me and he is eighty miles away. So far I have only seen their signatures at the bottom of their letters."

Machebeuf's letters give a detailed picture of missionary life in pre-Civil War America. He tells of visiting places which are now large cities: to Sandusky to find a gang of Irish laborers; to Toledo, "a real mudhole, on the banks of the Maumee. It consisted of a few frame houses, some log cabins . . . a large number of persons sick with Maumee fever. There were a few Catholic families and five or six single men. I said Mass for eight or ten persons in the frame shanty of a poor Canadian. There were a few other families along the river or in the country, so I remained for a few days to give them a chance to hear Mass and go to confession." In 1841 he was moved to a new parish in Lower Sandusky (which later became Fremont), a village on the Sandusky River. He had to care for Irish laborers who were digging the Erie Canal about fifty miles west. Included in his parish was Sandusky, a village on Lake Erie. Besides the Irish, his parish numbered German settlers and older Canadian families.

In his new post he was able to exchange visits with his old friend Father Lamy. Machebeuf did not stay at Lower Sandusky too long, recognizing — correctly — that Sandusky on the lake had a better chance for growth. Lower Sandusky was in a hollow, subject to fevers. Sandusky had better air. A letter home about this time tells of his joy that a railroad was at last approaching the area and due for completion to Cincinnati within two years, thus cutting to a day and night a trip that took him six days. The railroad would also connect him with New York. A neighboring priest in this period was Father John N. Neumann, who was later to become bishop of Philadelphia and whose holiness would lead to canonization in 1977. Machebeuf also began studying German because it "would be useful to me." The United States was in a great depression at this time, the people were unable to give much support, and his building program was in debt. He went to Canada to seek help from French Canadians.

In 1846 Father Machebeuf wrote home: "A few years ago I came to Sandusky as poor as Job, having neither church nor presbytery, nor ground to put them on. Today, we have a beautiful church of stone, a presbytery of twelve rooms, a cemetery of two acres, and a school for boys beside the church . . . and not a cent of debt on any of it." He confided that he was getting ready to build a free school and orphan asylum for which he had Sisters of Charity, and a boarding school for young ladies. The missioner was settling into parochial life. He received a visit from Father Pierre Jean De Smet, the famed missioner to the Indians of the Northwest. De Smet told the French priest of the harvest of souls waiting in the West. Once again the missionary urge began to burn in Machebeuf. He wrote to Lamy about the new challenge.

Father Lamy hurried to Sandusky. He told his friend: "When we left France, we made an agreement that we would keep together as much possible. So if you go, I shall have to follow you." Machebeuf realized that Lamy was ready to sacrifice his own work in Kentucky to which he was deeply committed. It was more than he could ask, so he put the notion of Oregon aside.

But God evidently had His own plans. In 1849 the American bishops had petitioned what was then called the Congregation of Propaganda to create a vicariate of New Mexico, a region that would embrace the present states of New Mexico, Utah, and parts of Colorado and Arizona. Although the United States had annexed the area some years earlier, the Church there was still being governed from Mexico — an unsatisfactory arrangement for the American military and one which left the old Spanish parishes without much supervision, resulting in laxity and abuses. Rome saw the wisdom of the American request and created the new ecclesiastical jurisdiction, naming Father John Lamy as vicar apostolic. The new bishop reminded his friend Father Machebeuf of their old agreement to stay together, adding, "They wish I should be Vicar Apostolic and I wish you to be my Vicar General, and from these two vicars we will try to make one good pastor."

Machebeuf was torn. He wrote to his brother and sister: "Ever since the time I saw the celebrated Father De Smet, I never got the thought of the Western missions out of my head. I could not forget his many efforts and entreaties to induce me to follow him to the Rocky Mountains. . . . Now, after two months of fighting, first with doubt and uncertainty, and then with all sorts of difficulties, I have left my dear Sandusky. I can hardly think of it without tears, not of regret, for I believe it was for the greater glory of God, but [because] the separation was too painful." He had decided to go with his friend to start anew, and his own bishop had reluctantly released him.

The usual way to Mexico was through Independence, Missouri, and then over the Santa Fe Trail. But Bishop Lamy chose to take a southern route because he wanted to stop in New Orleans to raise funds among the French there. From Louisiana they sailed to Galveston, Texas, then overland to San Antonio. In San Antonio they had to wait for a government train, so Father Machebeuf spent the time studying Spanish. It was the middle of May before the caravan was formed to make the thousand-mile journey. The caravan consisted of two hundred government wagons, each drawn by six mules — twenty-five wagons belonging to merchants and civilians — and a company of U.S. Army cavalry. Ahead lay desert, a scarcity of water, and hostile Indians. It took six weeks to reach El Paso, "the only Mexican town we saw, and that was not worthy of any special notice." After leaving El Paso the route went through La Jornada del Muerto (The Journey of the Dead), "a formidable desert, where along the road the bleaching bones of mules and horses testify to the danger to be apprehended from the want of water and pasture, and many human bones likewise tell their tale of Indian slaughter and assault." However, once that nightmare ended, the wagon train entered the Rio Grande Valley where water and fresh provisions could be obtained.

154

Perhaps if Bishop Lamy had not been wedded to Santa Fe by the Holy See, he might have thrown up his hands and retreated to Ohio. What the two priests found there was an ecclesiastical mess. Half the clergy of New Mexico had left the area for Mexico rather than live under American rule. Those who remained were strongly prejudiced against the newcomers. They had been governed by the bishop of Durango, fifteen hundred miles away, discipline was lax, and there was no apostolic spirit among either clergy or people. Most of the people were peons, living in practical slavery to the land owners. "In a population of 70,000," Father Machebeuf wrote, "there are but fifteen priests, and six of these were worn out by old age and have no energy. The others have not a spark of zeal, and their lives are scandalous beyond description. . . . The people show the best dispositions. They have the docility of children toward the priest." He observes that it would be the easiest thing to bring the people to full life in the faith and adds, "But alas! the great obstacle does not come from the people but from the priests themselves, who do not want the Bishop, for they dread a reform in their morals."

Despite the difficulties, Machebeuf was enchanted with Santa Fe. He studied its history, wrote about "The Palace" (the government building erected when Jamestown had not yet been founded), and thrilled to the sound of the bell in the ancient San Miguel Church, "the sweetest-toned bell in America." He reveled in the scenery and pointed out that "it would require the poetic temperament of Father De Smet to appreciate it fully and describe it. . . . I am now quite accustomed to scaling the mountain heights and crossing the winding streams, but I have not the grand and beautiful boats as once upon the Ohio, only a pair of Mexican ponies with no poetry in them."

In her famed book *Death Comes for the Archbishop*, Willa Cather tells how Bishop Lamy struggled to bring order out of religious chaos. Actually, it was Machebeuf who carried the heavier load. As a biographer puts it, "Bishop Lamy had told Father Machebeuf that he wished him to come with him to New Mexico 'to share his burdens,' and as Vicar General he had a share in them all. In some cases the share equaled the whole, and such burdens were generally the most disagreeable." Six weeks after their arrival in Santa Fe, Bishop Lamy went off to see the bishop of Durango and did not return until Christmas. Father Machebeuf, who was in charge, realized that he had become a real missioner again. Then the bishop was off to the Plenary Council of Baltimore and Machebeuf was alone again to work out the problems of the vicariate. Lamy brought back Sisters of Loretto with him and a new era was beginning.

Bishop Lamy gave his friend the task of reforming the Mexican priests. Father Machebeuf went to Albuquerque where a Padre José Gallegos was giving scandal. The Mexican priest was popular but was mainly noted for his dancing, gambling, and drinking. When the padre opposed Machebeuf, the latter read him out of his church. The Mexican priest went into the neighboring *aldeas* (villages) and aroused the people. These people descended on Albuquerque and ordered the Frenchman out of town. Machebeuf naturally refused and threats were made against his safety. The prefect, who heard of the "invasion," ordered the arrest of the troublemakers; but Father Machebeuf persuaded the official to withdraw the charges. The next day was Sunday, and when he appeared for Mass "everyone I met saluted me with apparently greater respect than ever. There were only three men from Albuquerque who took part in the rebellion; all the rest were from the Ranchos or villages on the lands of the rich proprietors. From that moment the Padre lost all hope of driving me away, and, abandoning the Church, he went into politics. . . , getting himself elected to the Congress of the United States as the Delegate from the Territory of New Mexico."

Bishop John Lamy was off again to Europe to make his obligatory *ad limina* visit to Rome and promote recruitment. With only one other priest in Santa Fe, Father Machebeuf had not only to care for the spiritual needs of that place but pay a monthly visit to Albuquerque and care for the needs of the extensive vicariate. When Lamy returned with three new priests, Machebeuf went to Independence, Missouri, to meet and escort back a new band of Sisters, during which trip he had to get them safely through a hostile band of Indians. The priest had no fear of Indians, saying always, "The Indians would never hurt me."

On one trek, he was passing through Apache Canyon, ahead of his party. The Indians had killed several soldiers in the area only a few days before. Machebeuf reached the top of the canyon, only to discover that the stage station there was under attack. He rode forward and an Indian chief came out to meet him.

"Are you Captain?" asked the chief.

"No Captain," said the priest, showing his crucifix.

"You Padre?"

"Yes, I'm Padre."

The chief called the other Indians to him and they all shook hands with Father Machebeuf. The chief asked the priest if he had seen any soldiers. Machebeuf told him that there were soldiers coming up the hill behind them.

"Adios, Padre!" cried the Indians as they mounted and made off. Machebeuf rode on to the relay station where he found three besieged Americans, grateful for their lives.

According to another story, Father Machebeuf was camped one morning on the plains when a band of Indians rode up. They expected the same hospitality that they would give if a stranger came into one of their villages. The missioner fed them what he could. The head of the band kept insisting what a great friend he was of the white men. He pulled from a pouch a paper he had received when he had acted as scout for the army and proudly showed it to the priest. It read: "I hereby certify that the bearer is the biggest thief unhung, and I warn all who read this paper to be on guard against him." The Indian asked the padre if he would add his own recommendation. Machebeuf wrote: "I have met the person described in the forgoing, and I have found no need to dispute the truth of the above declaration, or the necessity of the warning." The incident illustrates the missioner's quick wit and sense of humor.

Father Machebeuf also covered the Taos area. The pastor there had been Father Antonio Martínez, a talented man with little love for Anglos. Martínez had previously been a married man with a wife and daughter, both of whom had died. He then became a priest and was assigned to the Taos parish from which the Spanish Franciscans had withdrawn when Spain left Mexico. He opened a school and brought in a printing press to produce catechisms, schoolbooks, and the first newspaper to be published in New Mexico. He was suspected of being one of the instigators of the Taos uprising in 1847, when Governor Charles Bent and some fifteen others were killed by Mexicans and Indians in an attempt to drive out the Americans. The link could not be proved, so that fact and his political connections saved Martínez from arrest by the U.S. Army. Ten years later Martínez asked to resign, pleading ill health; Bishop Lamy replaced him with a Spanish priest whom he had recruited in Europe.

The Spanish priest, like many before him, considered himself superior to the Mexicans. Friction developed and Father Martínez set up an independent church, attracting not only many relatives but others who had looked up to him. Efforts at reconciliation failed and Father Machebeuf was sent to excommunicate the rebellious padre. Machebeuf's arrival in Taos was met with open threats against his person. Some non-Mexican members of the parish — Kit Carson, Ceran St. Vrain, and others, who like Carson had lost relatives in the Taos massacre — let the Martínez forces know that that previous incident would never be repeated and that Machebeuf was under their protection. Carson said, "We shall not let them do what they did in '47. I am a man of peace and my motto is: Good will to all. But I can fight a little yet, and I know of no better cause to fight for than my family, my Church and my friend Señor Vicario." Father Machebeuf carried out the excommunication without incident but remarked at the end, "It is always the way. I am the one sent to whip the cats."

To the north of New Mexico was a largely unexplored area which we now know as Colorado. The first

American to explore the region was Zebulon Pike; in 1806 he discovered a mountain, which was named after him: Pike's Peak (now spelled with the apostrophe dropped — Pikes Peak). John C. Frémont led another expedition in 1843. There were a few whites in the region, married to Indians, who lived by fur trapping. According to one historian of that period, a party of Cherokee Indians returning to their homes in Georgia discovered gold in a river, a few miles west of the present city of Denver. When they reached their homes, word of their discovery got out. A party of Georgians, under the leadership of Green Russell, set out in quest of the precious metal. They reached the area — Pike's Peak, which in this case loosely referred to almost all of Colorado and not the mountain — and after many failures Russell struck it big in a run leading into Cheery Creek. News of the strike reached Kansas and then moved eastward. Soon a mad rush was on. Gold was found in all sorts of places throughout the mountains, and camps were set up with such names as Deadwood, Carson City, Spanish Bar, Gold Dirt, Central City, Montezuma, Boulder, Denver City, Nevada City, and Buckskin Joe. In their search for the mother lode, silver was discovered and more prospectors poured in and set up new camps.

The many Catholics among the newcomers were priestless. Pike's Peak belonged to "the Vicariate Apostolic of the Territory East of the Rockies," whose head, Bishop John Miège, resided in Leavenworth, Kansas, six hundred miles away. Miège consulted the archbishop of St. Louis, saying that he had no priests to send to Pike's Peak and the intervening prairie was full of hostile Indians. Miège suggested that it would make better sense to have Pike's Peak cared for from Santa Fe; besides, there were some Mexican villages in the south, already responsible to Santa Fe.

So it happened. When word of the new addition reached Santa Fe, Bishop Lamy sent for his trouble-shooter. "There is only one thing to be done," he told Father Machebeuf. "I do not like parting from you but you are the man for Pike's Peak." Thus in late September of 1860, Machebeuf — accompanied by John Raverdy, a priest ordained only a couple of months earlier — set out for Pike's Peak with a wagon and light carriage (full of Mass necessities, bedding, and personal belongings) pulled by four mules. They camped along the way. When they reached Pueblo, they found a few Mexican families and paused to witness marriages and conduct baptisms. The next stop was the gold camp at Colorado City. They were advised to make Denver City their base, so they went there. They found Denver to be a town of three thousand people, of whom some two hundred were Catholics. They pitched their tent in a lot and set up shop.

Father Machebeuf's first task was to get a church. He had a small brick building under roof by Christmas. At its rear was a wooden shed — thirty feet long by twelve feet wide — which served as the rectory for himself and his companion. Father Raverdy, who spoke Spanish, was put in charge of the Mexican settlements to the south, while the pastor surveyed the scattered gold camps. Machebeuf noted the scarcity of women and already-abandoned mines. Towns grew up overnight and disappeared as quickly when the gold ran out. At this time, mining was done by the placer method (washing the gold from the sands of creeks); when this was exhausted, the miners sought the lode mines, veins from which the nuggets had come. Everything was quite transitory, making mission work difficult. However, some of the centers like Denver, Central City, Pueblo, and Colorado City seemed to be developing into permanent settlements. Machebeuf wrote to his brother at this time: "Besides the principal parish, established at Denver, we have begun another in the center of the mountains forty miles from here at a place called Central City. Next Sunday I shall go there and say Mass for the first time in our temporary church. After a few days I shall set out on my eighth trip across the South and Middle Parks. Although I have to cross the highest range of mountains several times to visit our poor Catholics who are almost buried alive in the depths of the mines, I have always preserved my good health. In crossing the Snowy Range I can see through the gorges far off into the Territory of Utah where the Mormons live, and in my trips through the parks and to California Gulch I often sleep under the stars, and sometimes in the midst of snow." Being a Rocky Mountain missioner was not an easy life.

Changes began to take place and the mission moved with them. The name Pike's Peak was replaced by the name Colorado. People began settling in the valleys, not to mine but to farm. A stability was coming to the region. Permanent churches were built, schools opened, a cemetery acquired. At the Plenary Council in Baltimore in 1866, Bishop Lamy recommended that Colorado be created as a vicariate. The hierarchy agreed and the petition was sent to Rome. On March 3, 1868, Propaganda announced the erection of the vicariate of Colorado. Father Joseph Machebeuf was named its vicar apostolic.

Machebeuf chose to be consecrated by his spiritual father, Archbishop Purcell, in Cincinnati. He used the trip also to try to raise funds for his growing territory, as he was deeply in debt (having bought properties for future Church development, which he anticipated would expand when a railroad reached Denver). His old parish in Sandusky raised just under two hundred dollars for him; but elsewhere the results were meager, as post-Civil War taxes were hurting everyone. He went back to Colorado with six hundred dollars he had raised and one priest recruit to add to the three he had; but the new man was to last only a year before he decided that Colorado was too difficult.

Bishop Machebeuf now took on a new role. He was no longer a missioner but an administrator and builder. The days on the trail were over. He set about erecting institutions to care for the new Catholics who were arriving. Because of his efforts, in 1887 the vicariate was made into the diocese of Denver, embracing all of Colorado, and he was named Denver's first bishop. Early the following year, his schoolmate and companion of many years — Archbishop John Lamy — died. He hurried to Santa Fe and at the funeral spoke through his tears, opining that his own end could not be far off. Later that year he went to Washington for a meeting and the laying of the cornerstone of the Catholic University, and for the first time felt weak from a journey. He made one more pastoral trip, returning to Denver on July 3, 1889. He was suffering from dysentery he had picked up and went to a room he kept at St. Vincent's Orphanage. Once there, he grew weaker and on July 10 died peacefully.

A biographer of Bishop Machebeuf, summing up this frontier missioner's life, tells us: "When Father Machebeuf came to Colorado in 1860 he was alone with Father Raverdy, without a single church, or roof over his head; when he was made bishop he had but three priests within his jurisdiction; when he died the Diocese of Denver counted 64 priests, 102 churches and chapels, 9 academies, 1 college, 1 orphan asylum, 1 house of refuge, 10 hospitals, and over 3,000 children in Catholic schools." The writer omits the hundred Sisters at work in the diocese.

With Joseph Projectus Machebeuf's death an era also ended — the era of the emigrés. American Catholicism will always be indebted to the men and women who left comfortable homes in France and other European countries for the loneliness and hardship of the American wilderness. Their monuments are the dioceses reaching from the Appalachians to the Rockies. Where there was a need in a growing nation, they were ready to fill it without counting the cost.

# *PART FOUR*

## The Irish Brigade □ *INTRODUCTION*

The nineteenth century witnessed an outstanding group of American Catholic churchmen. They came to prominence at a time when the Church was expanding and sinking roots. Cultured men, well educated, sometimes autocratic, they governed their dioceses with a strong hand — and their influence was as much national as it was local. Some names come to mind: Fenwick, Kenrick, Ireland, Purcell, the Spaldings, Hughes, McCloskey, O'Connell, Kenna, McQuaid. All had roots in Ireland and they put an Irish stamp upon the Church which was sometimes good and sometimes bad, in that Germans and Italians and others were often alienated. The schismatic Polish National Church says that it arose out of the intransigence of Irish pastors.

Nevertheless, the members of the Irish Brigade were given a job to do at a critical point in the development of American Catholicism and they did it well. They erected parishes, built schools and colleges, founded hospitals and other institutions of charity, opened seminaries, developed the Sisterhood, and were largely instrumental in creating the Church as we know it today.

# CHAPTER 11

## *Peer of Prelates*

### *John England*

There was an old history professor, since gone to that region where history does not exist, who found John England amusing because of his name. "England," he would say. "What a strange name for an Irishman." Considering the low regard held in Ireland for England, it was an odd name for an Irishman and a Corkman at that. But England the Irishman was destined to become an American and a bishop in a strongly Protestant area whose deeds would rank so favorably when compared with his contemporaries that the historian Peter Guilday would write, "John England was the peer of all these prelates."

John England was born in Cork, Ireland, on September 23, 1786. He was a brilliant youth and at the age of fourteen began the study of law, a vocation in which his debating and argumentative skills would have stood him in good stead. However, two years later — in 1802 — he switched careers and entered St. Patrick's College in Carlow to prepare for the priesthood. He was ordained in 1808 and, since he was only twenty-two at the time, had to get a dispensation from Rome. Despite his comparative youth, he was given many responsibilities because of his many talents. A good writer who was fond of books, he organized a parish circulating library and began the *Religious Repository*, a Catholic monthly. His belief in a Catholic press was to continue until his death. He was appointed superintendent of the diocesan seminary and instructor of philosophy and theology, secretary of the diocese, inspector of city schools, and secretary of the personnel board that examined candidates to the priesthood. The Irish patriot Daniel O'Connell persuaded him to accept the trusteeship of Cork's *Mercantile Chronicle* (an antigovernment paper). He wrote and published a text called *School Primer of Irish History*. He gained a reputation throughout Ireland for his fearless speeches and was regarded as a leading defender of Irish rights and Irish justice.

While John England was growing in stature in Irish eyes, across the sea the infant Church in America was struggling. Ambrose Maréchal had been appointed third bishop of Baltimore and his widespread diocese extended south to Florida. Because of the distances involved, he could not give it the supervision it required. In Charleston, South Carolina, two Irish priests named Gallagher and Browne — rebellious and troublesome — refused to obey the archbishop's orders and caused what was called the Charleston schism. Browne, the real instigator, had gone so far as to propose to a priest in Ireland that he go to Utrecht and be consecrated by an Old Catholic bishop (a device that has been used off and on since then to get valid if illicit orders) and come to Charleston to establish the Independent Catholic Church of the United States, free of the tyranny of the "French Junta." With both sides appealing to Rome, the situation had become increasingly complicated. Archbishop Maréchal wrote to Rome that distance compounded the problem and that it would be best for the Southland to have its own bishop. He recommended that North Carolina, South Carolina, and Georgia be formed into one diocese with its center at Charleston, South Carolina. Maréchal also proposed that the Jesuit Father Benedict Fenwick, whom he had sent to Charleston to solve the problem, be made its first bishop.

Why Rome accepted only half of Maréchal's proposal is not known; but on July 12, 1820, Pope Pius VII erected the diocese of Charleston and instead of Fenwick appointed John England of Cork, Ireland, as Charleston's first bishop. The selection of this unknown man was a disappointment to Maréchal who believed that an outsider was not going to understand the problems he faced. Also unknown was how Rome selected England. Possibly the Holy See was watching him as a comer in the Irish Church and quite possibly some Irish cleric in Rome recommended England to the Congregation for the Propagation of the Faith which had jurisdiction over the United States. At any event, England was chosen and privately instructed to bring "peace and order" to his new diocese and settle the problem of trusteeism which was causing havoc not only in Charleston but elsewhere. (Trusteeism is a term meaning "control of parishes by laymen that is over and above what ecclesiastical law allows.")

England was consecrated a bishop in the Cork cathedral on September 21, 1820. A month later he sailed on the long journey to Charleston, arriving there December 31. Charleston at this time was the most important political and social center in the South. The city was surrounded by large plantations on which lived nineteen thousand slaves; indeed, the last slave ship to the United States had docked at Charleston only twelve years earlier. The city itself had about thirty-eight thousand people. Catholics were few, thirty-six hundred in the whole new diocese, and often discriminated against. The Charleston gentry received the new bishop courteously but without enthusiasm. They saw a man of medium height with strong facial features who chose to remain beardless in a city of beards. But what surprised many who ranked Catholics at the bottom of the cultural ladder was that the new bishop was a man of refinement, intelligence, and education. He might well fit into what was called the "City of Gentlemen."

Within a week after taking possession of his diocese, the first bishop of Charleston delivered a pastoral letter to his flock. It was an innovation for American dioceses and it was well thought out, probably the result of the long voyage across the Atlantic. He stressed the validity of ecclesiastical authority as having been established by Christ, an indirect reference to the trustee problem. He cautioned his flock about too great a trust in worldly things because no one knew when he would be called to the judgment seat of God. He issued a ruling ending reserved pews in churches, thus making both rich and poor equal in the house of God. Then he made two visitations, first around his diocese, which consisted of North and South Carolina and Georgia, and then to his neighboring bishops to the north. As a result of his visits, he wrote Archbishop Maréchal suggesting the calling of a national synod to deal with trusteeism and other problems. Maréchal, still miffed because England had been chosen over his own candidate, ignored the request. Bishop England also realized the need for an American edition of the English Missal for use by the faithful at Mass and asked for suggestions. Maréchal was again silent.

England approached the trustee problem in his own diocese obliquely. Of the two priests who were making trouble, he gladly gave one permission to withdraw from the diocese and the other he transferred to Savannah. The laymen — who controlled St. Mary's Church, which was serving as the cathedral — were not attacked directly. He built a temporary chapel and bought a house nearby, moving there from St. Mary's. Neither he nor any other priest would offer Mass at the old church. This left the trustees with an empty building. "It is folly to attempt raising the edifice of Catholicity upon Calvinistic foundations," he told them. The other properties of the diocese were transferred to the bishop's name, but the St. Mary trustees held firm.

Trusteeism was a peculiarity and affliction of the Church in young America. It had its roots in Protestantism and the new sense of democracy, and was even supported by civil law which had no consideration of hierarchy as it exists in the Catholic Church. Protestant congregations owned their churches and could hire or fire pastors at will. Churches were set up as private, independent corporations through acts of state legislatures. The liberation of the United States from England created heady times, and citizens who had acquired the right to vote and elect their own civic officers transferred these civil powers to other areas of their lives. Some Catholics sought to apply this freedom to their own churches, and this new trusteeism was creating problems in such diverse places as New York and Charleston.

The matter came to a head in Charleston when the trustees presented a bill to the state legislature that would prevent any change in the parish's charter. Bishop England appeared before the House of Representatives in Columbia and spoke against the measure. Realizing that they were outmaneuvered and that they held nothing but an empty church, the Charleston trustees yielded. Thus ended the Charleston schism. St. Mary's was reopened and used once again as the cathedral. When Archbishop Maréchal died, Bishop England renewed his plea for a synod with the new archbishop, James Whitfield. In one of his first acts, Archbishop Whitfield convened the First Provincial Council, which in one of its decrees stated: "Since lay-trustees have too often abused the power given them by the civil law to the great detriment of religion and not without scandal to the faithful, we very greatly desire that in the future no church shall be built or consecrated unless it shall have been assigned by written instrument to the bishop in whose diocese it is to be built, wherever this can be done." Thus John England not only played a significant role in ending the trustee problems but also was greatly responsible for the American councils which would follow, thus anticipating the collegiality and importance of national hierarchies which would come many years later.

Bishop England rejoiced when a railroad was opened between Charleston and Augusta because it made travel in his big diocese easier. Charleston was a travel center for the South. There was a regular stage to Boston, eleven days away. A packet boat was scheduled to New York. Another ship went to Wilmington, North Carolina, where by stage and rail one could get to Norfolk and a boat across the bay to Baltimore. Bishop England made an annual trip around his own diocese; but he frequently journeyed outside his diocese on business, to give lectures, and to consult with other bishops. Four times he crossed the Atlantic to raise money and personnel for his diocese.

These trips provided fuel for anti-Catholic diatribes, averring that the bishop was getting instructions from the papacy, receiving foreign funds to overthrow the country, and encouraging "foreign turbulence imported by the shipload" to support "priest-controlled machines."

Anti-Catholicism was a problem for the bishop from the time he arrived in his diocese. Although he was ecumenical before the term was invented and won the respect of many Protestant leaders, anti-Catholicism was almost endemic in the national character — and until the new national constitution legislated religious freedom, there were laws in many states disenfranchising Catholics or even exiling them. This discrimination was kept alive by a raft of books, some from England, some native: *Master Key to Popery; Female Convents: Secrets of Nunneries Disclosed; Jesuit Juggling: Forty Popish Frauds*, to mention but a few. To these books must be added the Protestant publications which proclaimed the republic to be threatened by Roman Catholics: the *Southern Religious Telegraph* (Richmond); *The Protestant*, founded to defend the Gospel from popery and "to exhibit those doctrines and practices of Roman Catholics which are contrary to the interests of mankind"; *The Gospel Advocate*, *New Age*, and *The Converted Catholic* all thrived on anti-Catholic verbal abuse. Fired by these publications, Protestant pastors mounted their pulpits to roar that American citizenship and Roman Catholicism were incompatible and that Catholics should stay out of politics. It only added fuel to the fire when on February 6, 1826, after his five-year residence, Bishop England took the oath of American citizenship.

While these seeds of the Know-Nothing movement

were being sown, Bishop England was not inactive. He rose to the defense of his faith on pulpits and stages and even in the halls of Congress. His sermons and speeches would often run two hours, yet he held his audiences enthralled. Not too many of these talks remain because he did not use prepared texts but spoke extemporaneously from his heart and deep knowledge. A two-hour talk in Boston, "On American Citizenship," was hailed as brilliant and eloquent by the Boston *Transcript* which summarized it as "intensely imbued with the pure and holy spirit of Heaven-born charity and kindness." His theme was that the Catholic Church preached the religion given to the world by Jesus Christ and that it had preserved the principles of common law that were the principles of republican government. Roman Catholics made the best citizens, the bishop went on to say, because the freedom of republicanism was natural to them. Through his talks he became the leading apologist for Catholicism and a man nationally known.

Bishop England was also a strong believer in the axiom *"Scriptum manet"* ("Writing endures"). Because of his journalistic experiences in Ireland, he was surprised to find that in America there was no Catholic press, particularly when the Protestants were so amply blessed with publications of their own. Moreover, he didn't find a conviction on the part of bishops that Catholics needed a press. In 1809 Father Gabriel Richard had started a small publication, *Michigan Essay and Impartial Observer;* but it had little circulation, was limited to Michigan, appeared spasmodically, and played second fiddle to the production of catechisms and texts. To Father Richard's credit was the importation of the first press west of the Alleghenies and the foundation of the first paper in Michigan. Bishop England had something else in mind. He envisioned a paper that would be national in scope, appear weekly, have strong apologetic overtones to answer the many calumnies being spread about the Church, teach Catholic doctrine, and give news about the Catholic Church that was not only national but international.

Bishop England found support for his idea in Judge William Gaston, of New Bern, North Carolina, the most celebrated member of his flock. Judge Gaston was the son of a prominent physician who had been killed by Tories for his support of the American Revolution. The judge had graduated from Princeton and he had educated his own children in Emmitsburg, Maryland — his son at Mount St. Mary's with the Sulpicians and his daughters with Mother Seton. He had served in the North Carolina Senate and in the United States Congress. Although North Carolina was the most anti-Catholic state in the Union, Judge Gaston did not hide his Catholicism and he had a reputation for defending minority causes. He was impressed with the new bishop of Charleston and the two men became good friends. Judge Gaston made a generous loan to the bishop so that the new paper could get started.

The debut issue of *United States Catholic Miscellany* appeared on June 5, 1822, the first Catholic weekly in the United States. Bishop England told his readers that the paper would be noted for its "candor, moderation, fidelity, charity and diligence." But Bishop England was to learn that a good idea is not enough, that one has to sell it. Circulation came slowly, and there were two brief suspensions when money ran out. With the third start-up, the paper appeared regularly until two factors — the Civil

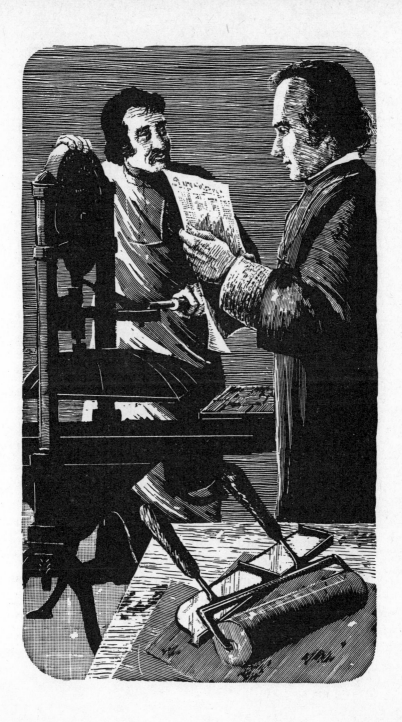

War and a disastrous fire — caused its demise in 1861. The bishop used the paper to defend the Church against the many attacks made on it, and if a criticism can be made of the paper, it is that at times the *Catholic Miscellany* seemed more to address Protestants than Catholics. But it was a voice badly needed for its time, and it did have a strong effect on fair-minded people. As a publisher, England also printed tracts and pamphlets and brought out the first missal for the laity in the United States.

Early in his bishopric, England had made a courtesy call on President James Monroe and his secretary of state, John Quincy Adams (who was to become sixth president of the United States). Adams, like his father, had an inborn New England dislike for Catholicism. He had delivered a Fourth of July address that year, full of digs at the Catholic Church which he called "that pretentious system of despotism and superstition which, in the name of a meek and humble Jesus, has been spread over the Christian world." Several years later Bishop England was in Washington and invited to speak in St. Patrick's Church. He used the occasion to rebut Adams's Fourth of July oration, even though Adams was now president. But Adams, ever a politician, did not take the rebuttal amiss. He met England at a reception a few days later and — as the bishop later reported to Judge Gaston — the president received him "in a very flattering manner, & upon arrival at home found a card for dinner on the succeeding Saturday. We had much conversation on several topics, & a little about yourself, in which he appeared to think it news that you were a Popish church warden."

On that same trip Bishop England was invited to speak to the Congress of the United States, the first Catholic clergyman so honored. He arrived at the podium to find a packed house, including President Adams. He did not temper or compromise his remarks because of his audience, even beginning his two-hour talk by blessing himself. He addressed two questions: "Can a free government possibly exist with the Roman Catholic religion?" and "Can a good Roman Catholic be a loyal American citizen?" It was a brilliant talk. He told his listeners that if the Catholic Church was what they believed it to be, he himself would not be a Catholic. "You have no power to interfere with my religious rights," he told Congress, "and the tribunal of the Church has no power to intervene with my civil rights." He said that of all citizens, none were "more free to think and act for themselves on our rights" than Catholics. He added, "I would not allow to the pope, or to any bishop of our church outside this Union, the smallest interference with the humblest vote at our most insignificant ballot box." He lauded the principle of separation of Church and State provided for by the Constitution. Bishop England believed and stated that the Catholic Church was the one institution which had preserved down through the ages the principles that created English liberty and that the Church was the mother of republicanism. But one speech before Congress would not change the national mood, and Bishop England was to do battle with anti-Catholicism all his episcopal life.

Some have criticized Bishop England for not taking a strong stand against slavery. "I have been asked by many," he once said, "whether I am friendly to the existence or continuation of slavery. I am not. But I also see the impossibility of now abolishing it here. When it can and ought to be abolished is a question for the legislature and not for me." There are some who say that he identified himself too closely with the South, but the South was where he lived and governed and served his people. He was also turned off by the abolitionists — Northern fanatics, he believed — who were as much anti-Catholic as they were antislavery. He thought of those people as busybodies who should allow the South to settle its own problems. He also regarded the abolitionists, largely New Englanders, as hypocrites who had been enriched by the slave trade and who were still carrying it on illicitly. In the *Miscellany* he wrote: "We have had given to us the names of zealous and noisy abolitionists at the North, who we are told, make largely at the present day by the traffic. We have ourselves seen in ports in the United States, within ten years, several vessels fitted out evidently for this trade, and notoriously employed in it, and owned by our Northern merchants, but against which legal proof could not be exhibited."

Although the bishop's approach to the slavery question was one of moderation, he was often condemned by both sides, simply because he was a Catholic. In 1833 Pope Gregory XVI appointed him a papal envoy to go to Haiti and report on the state of the Church there. The abolitionists drew up a petition asking President Jean Pierre Boyer of Haiti not to receive the bishop because he was not averse to Southern slavery and was therefore an enemy of black people. Southerners criticized the bishop because he was dealing with the black president as an equal, which was what he did consider him. Actually, England went out his way to be a friend to black people. South Carolina law prohibited the education of slaves, so the bishop opened a school for free Negroes, using two students from a seminary he had begun and two Ursuline Sisters from a community he had brought to the diocese as teachers. Many of these freed blacks had been Catholics but had fallen away. Within a month of the school's opening, eighty-four children and many of their parents had returned to the sacraments. He regularly said his Sunday Mass for blacks and every Sunday evening the cathedral was reserved for black instruction.

Bishop England maintained a hectic schedule because he was in great demand as a speaker. He once described himself "as having been in twenty-one states of the Union, in every description of society; in the city and in the forest, from the table of the President to the hut of the Indian; and having proclaimed the doctrines of [my] church in the halls of legislation, in the courts of justice, in the churches of those who opposed it, in the crowded steamboats of the Mississippi, and in the woods of Kentucky, to every description of hearers." All of this missionary work was not done without cost. In 1841 he made his last trip to Europe, appealing for financial aid, priests, and nuns. He returned in time for speaking engagements in the Philadelphia and Baltimore areas. Although he was only fifty-six, his hair had long before turned white, and when he reached Charleston, he felt expended and like an old man.

On the first Sunday of Lent, 1842, Bishop England said Mass for the last time. A great weakness had come over him and he wrote to the archbishop of Baltimore to alert him about the "precarious" state of his health. He instructed his chancellor to arrange the temporal affairs of the diocese "according to the laws of the State so that all things may be secure." On Sunday, April 10, a high Mass was offered in the Charleston cathedral for his recovery, and prayers were said in all the Episcopal churches in the city. On the preceding day he had been remembered in the Jewish synagogue. But in the early hours of Monday, April 11, he slipped away to God. The bells of the city tolled the dolorous news, and the city closed in mourning.

"In the death of Bishop England, true religion has lost a friend," eulogized the *Charleston Courier*. "He was distinguished for strength of mind, power of argument, deep and various learning, and a bold and impressive eloquence, and was justly ranked among the intellectual and literary ornaments of our city." His own paper summed it all up: "Every faculty of mind and body which he had received from his Maker he dedicated in life to His service, and he completed the oblation by dying the death of the missionary, death because of the zealous performance of his arduous duties."

# CHAPTER 12

## The American Cardinal

### James Gibbons

While it is not true that all comparisons are odious, it is a fact that most of them limp, since seldom are people or things equal enough to be compared and the result is that we usually end up differentiating between apples and oranges. Thus the question "Who was the greatest Catholic American churchman?" could have many responses. There were those who were great because of their pioneering spirit, great in their sanctity, great in organizational ability, great in their preaching, great in journalism, and so on down the line. But if only one name could be picked, I think it would have to be that of Cardinal James Gibbons, who came on the scene at a time of crucial growth and who was held in esteem both by Church and State, four popes, and a half dozen presidents — and whose wisdom and leadership were respected. His priesthood spanned the years beginning with the Civil War and extended through World War I. He was a bridge between America's past and its present who took the legacy of the eighteenth century and led his Church into the twentieth century. His life was marked by fortuitous circumstances as if one could see the hand of God at work.

James Gibbons was born in Baltimore, Maryland, on July 23, 1834, the first son and fourth child of Thomas and Bridget Gibbons. His parents had left Ireland some years earlier, going first to Canada where they found it was too cold, then settling in Baltimore where they became American citizens and Thomas Gibbons found good employment with a shipping concern. When Thomas's health began failing and doctors advised a change of climate, he and his wife decided to take their children — now numbering six — back to Ireland where they settled in County Mayo, bought a small farm, and opened a store. When he was seven, James began school and became an altar boy. The family was doing well until a double tragedy struck. First came the potato blight which led to the great Potato Famine that began a torrent of immigration to America; at the same time cholera broke out in County Mayo and Thomas Gibbons was one of its victims. The widow decided that Ireland held little promise for her orphaned children and decided — six years after her husband's death — to go back to America, this time to New Orleans. Thus at nineteen, James Gibbons returned to America and found work at three dollars a week to support his family. Again fate intervened, this time in the form of a yellow-fever epidemic (which was to claim the lives of ten percent of the Crescent City's population). Gibbons fell ill and for weeks hovered between life and death. During his recovery, he began to think of his life in terms of eternity and began to seriously ponder whether or not he was being called to the priesthood. The question was decided during a retreat he made, and a priest-friend advised him to go to the Sulpician Fathers in Baltimore. He applied to Archbishop Francis Kenrick of Baltimore, was accepted, and undertook the sixteen-day journey to his new home. For two years he studied at St. Charles College, the minor seminary at Ellicott City (where the property adjoined the Carroll estate). During his stay there,

Gibbons came to know Colonel Charles Carroll, the grandson of the signer of the Declaration of Independence. He did his last four years of preparation at St. Mary's Seminary on Paca Street in Baltimore, was ordained there by Archbishop Kenrick on June 30, 1861 (to the sounds of men marching off to the Civil War), and was assigned as curate at St. Patrick's Church.

Baltimore was badly divided at the time between Northern and Southern sympathizers. Young Gibbons had to make a choice and he did it in a way that would mark his future life — he thought the problem out. "I had been born a Southerner and brought up a Southerner and my heart was of course with the Southern states. Indeed my brother was actually fighting with the Confederate army," he wrote later. "But I could never believe that secession would succeed and even if it should, I could not help but see that it would be the destruction of what was already a growing and what might become a very great nation. Therefore my head was always with the Union." Nevertheless, besides caring for two mission churches, he served as military chaplain at Fort McHenry (a hospital and prison for Confederate captives). When Lincoln was shot after war's end, Gibbons observed, "His murder was the greatest misfortune which ever came upon the South."

Archbishop Kenrick had died during the war years and the new archbishop was Martin J. Spalding, who had been bishop of Louisville, Kentucky, when named. Spalding was from an old Maryland family and was well regarded among American bishops. The new archbishop cast his eye about his archdiocese, looking for a secretary, and his glance rested upon Father Gibbons. Thus, two months after the war had ended, the young priest found

185

himself part of the episcopal household, companion of the archbishop on his visitations, and confidant in matters of internal Church policies. He could not know it, of course; but his grooming for higher posts had started. One of his first tasks was to work on the organization of a plenary council which had been called for 1866. The council received wide publicity because it brought together bishops from the North and South in the unity of the Church, the first major meeting in which former enemies were joined in friendship. The occasion was considered so important that President Andrew Johnson was present for the opening ceremony. The council also gave Gibbons the opportunity to meet the American hierarchy which — as a result of the council — Gibbons would soon join.

Among the recommendations of the council to Rome was the division of the diocese of Charleston (North Carolina was to be split off as a vicariate). A *terna* — three suggestions for the new bishop — was sent to Rome, and Gibbons's name headed the list. Archbishop Spalding went to Rome on Church business and undoubtedly made a strong recommendation for his secretary. In any event the appointment was made and on August 16, 1868, at the age of thirty-four, Gibbons found himself consecrated as the youngest bishop in the world, although there could not have been many who envied him. The new vicariate of Wilmington embraced the whole state of North Carolina where, among its million people, there were only a handful of Catholics and a few priests. It was a mission territory in the truest sense.

Gibbons found Wilmington a place of total confusion. The state was in the process of Reconstruction, and illiterate former slaves made up the government. The war had left homes destroyed and farms ravaged. Public services had broken down, schools were closed, and carpetbaggers and other Northern profiteers were on hand to pick up the heirlooms of an impoverished people. Gibbons, shocked, described the actions of the North as "abominable perfidy." When he went to vote, the ex-slave in charge demanded he show his naturalization papers and prove he was a citizen. The bishop explained that he was born in the United States, but the black was unmoved. Then he remembered he had a document in Latin that contained his faculties of the Church, authorizing him to say Mass and celebrate the sacraments, and he showed this to the election official. The black man — unable to read, let alone recognize Latin — accepted the "evidence" and permitted Bishop Gibbons to vote.

The new bishop began the rounds of his vast territory, meeting Catholic families. This four-week journey took him from one end of the state to the other, baptizing and confirming. Everywhere he was well received. He discovered Catholics who had not seen a priest in years and he made converts. He began keeping a journal and, besides being a record of his activities, it is rich in Irish wit, relating the humorous incidents he experienced — and there were many, even if it meant telling stories on himself.

When one of his altar boys in Wilmington, Thomas Frederick Price, told him that he wanted to be a priest, Gibbons was overjoyed and helped the young man enter the seminary in Baltimore. Later, he would help Father Price when he, along with James Anthony Walsh, sought aid to begin the Catholic Foreign Mission Society of America, more popularly known as the Maryknoll Fathers.

It is a long way from the poverty of the piney woods of North Carolina to the splendor of the Vatican, but that was the journey the bishop of Wilmington was to make. Pope Pius IX sent out a call to all bishops to attend an ecumenical council to be held at the Vatican, the first ecumenical council since the Council of Trent. With bishops from all over the world in Rome, Gibbons clearly realized that he was part of a universal church. The meeting was an important one for Gibbons because it introduced him to leaders of the world Church, with many of whom he would later deal. The most important question Vatican Council I (December 1869 to July 1870) considered was papal infallibility. Many of the American bishops, while agreeing with the teaching, held that it was inopportune to define it, fearing that it would only increase anti-Catholicism back home. When the vote was finally taken after an exhausting debate of months, infallibility was approved 533-2, one of the holdouts being Bishop Edward Fitzgerald of Little Rock, Arkansas. With this question settled, Bishop Gibbons and the other Americans returned home. Back in North Carolina, he must have been struck by the contrast of the grandeur of Rome and the poverty of his own vicariate.

One day Bishop Gibbons was visiting with one of his priests when the talk turned to conversions. The bishop observed that what was needed was a book that presented Catholicism in a simple but complete way. "Why don't you write such a book?" the priest asked him. It was an apt question that sent the bishop to his desk and the result — in 1876 — was *The Faith of Our Fathers*, a book that went through edition after edition, was translated into many languages, sold in the millions, and only went out of print in recent years. Written simply and directly, it told the story of the Catholic faith in biblical terms and thus had a great appeal to Protestants and led to many conversions. Among those converted by the book was the daughter of Nathaniel Hawthorne — Rose Hawthorne Lathrop — who later became a Catholic nun, founder of a community devoted to the incurable sick. The book also contributed to the national reputation of its author who was revealed in its pages as a wise and learned man of great faith.

Not long after the return from Rome, the bishop of Richmond, John McGill, died. Archbishop Spalding, in failing health himself from throat cancer, appointed Bishop Gibbons administrator of the diocese and recommended to Rome that Gibbons be named bishop of the Virginia diocese. It was one of Spalding's last acts. Gibbons was summoned to the deathbed of his mentor and gave him the last rites of the Church. The eighth archbishop to be named to the see of Baltimore was James Roosevelt Bayley, bishop of Newark and an extraordinary man. Archbishop Bayley was a nephew of St. Elizabeth Seton and first cousin to James Roosevelt, the father of Franklin Delano Roosevelt (thirty-second president of the United States). Urbane and used to moving in high society, Archbishop Bayley had been an Episcopal minister and rector of the most fashionable church in New York City. He was converted to the Catholic Church in 1842. Being unmarried, he decided to stay in his career choice and went to St. Sulpice in Paris where he was ordained in 1844. He returned to the United States and took a vice-presidential post at Fordham University, then called St. John's College. Four years later he was appointed secretary to the bishop of New York. In 1853 Bayley was named first bishop of Newark (New Jersey) and remained there until his transfer to Baltimore in 1872 to succeed Archbishop Spalding.

Bishop Gibbons had become acquainted with Bayley at the Vatican Council, so when he learned of his appointment, he wrote to him of his delight. Archbishop Bayley, failing in health, replied that one of the consolations of going to Baltimore was that he would see more of Gibbons, adding, "I count on you as my right-hand man." The two men would be in adjoining dioceses, since the same ship that brought news of Bayley's appointment also brought confirmation of Gibbons's assignment to Richmond. When the new bishop of Richmond was installed on October 20, 1872, Archbishop Bayley presided and preached. The appointment to Richmond was not an exchange of one job for another. Rome left Gibbons still in charge of North Carolina, so it merely doubled his responsibility and work. He did get some help in the Tarheel State when he brought in the Benedictines to establish Belmont Abbey. Moreover, he was a frequent rider on the train to Baltimore when Archbishop Bayley was too ill to officiate. Among his converts in Richmond was John Bannister Tabb, whom he also helped to become a priest. Bayley meanwhile sent a request to Rome asking for a coadjutor and recommending Gibbons. The appointment was made in May of 1877, and Bishop Gibbons was back home where he had started out. On October 3 of that year Archbishop Bayley died and the young coadjutor became the "primate" of the United States. When the pallium — the stole of office — was placed over his shoulders, his seventy-three-year old mother sat among the dozen bishops that witnessed the ceremony in the Baltimore cathedral, the same cathedral where her son had been baptized forty-three years earlier and where he would rule for the next forty-odd years. The new archbishop was also to govern under a new pope. In less than two weeks after he had received the pallium, Gioacchino Vincenzo Pecci was elected pope and took the name of Leo XIII.

It was a time of great change for the universal Church and the Church in the United States. In Italy the Papal States had been lost to the Church and the pope had become "the prisoner of the Vatican." Yet, at the same time, European missioners were carrying Christianity into new lands in Africa, Asia, and Oceania — and often at the cost of their lives they were bringing armies of new converts into the ancient faith. In the United States rapid change was the order of the day. Waves of European immigrants were pouring through East Coast ports to find work in factories, mills, and mines, often in exploited conditions. Both city and rural populations were swelling, bringing new problems. Although the anti-Catholic spirit was strong, politicians wooed the new arrivals because of the voting power their numbers gave them. Unionism was being promoted secretly and beginning its growth. The Church had to meet these changing conditions by building new parishes and schools, by erecting hospitals and shelters for the needy, by expanding its human services. There was also an intellectual ferment in the Church, created by the writings of such men as Orestes Brownson and Isaac Hecker.

Gibbons brought a new, open style to the Baltimore see. Whereas previous bishops had bypassed the city of Washington to avoid the appearance of any political impropriety, Gibbons traveled frequently between Baltimore and the nation's capital, thirty-seven miles away. He accepted invitations to dinners and receptions and was soon well known to high figures in government and among the diplomats, who in turn cultivated the man whom they recognized as the leader of the American Church. This leadership was confirmed by the Holy See. One of Archbishop Gibbons's first important acts was to organize the Third Plenary Council which was to open November 9, 1884, at St. Mary's Seminary in Baltimore. It was customary for the pope to send a personal representative who would preside over the sessions. Leo XIII decided that instead of sending someone from Europe, he would name an American, and the person he chose was Archbishop Gibbons. There were many crucial problems facing the Church in the United States, and the bishops were of diverse opinions on what to do about them. In his role as chairman, Archbishop Gibbons guided the sessions wisely and prudently, with fairness and bits of humor to lighten heavy situations. The Third Baltimore Council was the most productive Catholic meeting ever held in the United States. It legislated days of fast and abstinence as well as holy days of obligation; ordered parochial schools; mandated a Catholic university; supported the Catholic press and even recommended a Catholic daily paper; organized mission work among Indians and blacks; directed the compilation of the Baltimore catechism for use in Catholic schools; and passed legislation affecting priests, parishes, and the laity.

Gibbons's growing prestige in the United States did not go unnoticed in Rome. As the spring of 1886 was slipping into summer, word came from Rome that Leo XIII had named the Baltimore prelate a cardinal. On June 30, the twenty-fifth anniversary of Gibbons's ordination, the red hat was bestowed on the new cardinal in a ceremony in the Baltimore cathedral. The Roman ceremony of installation would be delayed until the following year. The news was well received. *Harper's Weekly* (the *Time* and *Newsweek* of that day) reported: "Archbishop Gibbons is in his fifty-second year and while not physically strong is a hard worker, performing conscientiously all the duties of his exalted office. The cardinalate in the United States is an honor and very little more. He is best known to the reading public for his book *The Faith of Our Fathers*. He will be the honorary head of a Church of twelve archbishops, 62 bishops, 7,293 priests and seven million Catholics." The Baltimore newspapers were rhapsodic in describing their pleasure, referring to Gibbons proudly as "Our Cardinal."

The first big problem to face the new cardinal was what position he would take on the growing labor movement. For many years workingmen had been made to suffer the whims and greed of exploiting employers. Orestes Brownson had called the American workingmen slaves and had likened their condition to slavery in the South. Archbishop Spalding had declared: "Capital is a tyrant and labor is its slave." Yet not all bishops felt this way. Gibbons's predecessor had written: "These miserable associations called labor unions are subversive of government and communistic. No Catholic with any idea of the spirit of religion will encourage them." Moreover, Rome had forbidden Catholics to belong to secret societies, and the Knights of Labor was a secret group. The Knights — out of which was to come the American Federation of Labor — had been formed in 1869, and by the time Gibbons became cardinal it had grown to nearly three quarters of a million members. Since employers would fire anyone who belonged, membership was secret and great efforts were made to preserve that secrecy and guard its roster against company spies. The leader of the Knights was Terence Powderly, a Catholic from the Scranton coal mines, and three fourths of the membership belonged to the Catholic Church. Was the Church to condemn organized labor, ignore it, or give it support and assistance? This was the question facing Gibbons.

The matter came to a head in 1887 and coincided with Gibbons's journey to Rome to be installed as a cardinal. The Canadian bishops, three years earlier, had obtained from the Holy See a condemnation of the Knights of Labor. Catholics were ordered to resign or be excommunicated. Some American bishops interpreted Rome's earlier response to Canada as now equally applicable to the United States. In Maine, Bishop James Healy published the ban. Archbishop Michael Corrigan of New York declared, "The Knights are totally forbidden." Other bishops argued that the Vatican's reply to Canada did not affect the United States. Gibbons was disturbed because he saw the American bishops being maneuvered into a position of being "a friend to the powerful rich and an enemy to the helpless poor." He invited the archbishops of the United States to come to Baltimore for a meeting on the matter, and when they did he arranged for Terence Powderly to present labor's case to them. Gibbons made known his own position: condemnation of the Knights would be a disaster for the Church. He believed that if the Church cooperated with labor it could influence labor's course. Of the twelve archbishops at the meeting, ten sided with the cardinal and two opposed him. Gibbons decided that on the trip to Rome to receive his red robes he would take on the Holy Office itself and obtain a reversal.

Cardinal Gibbons sent two supporters ahead of him to Rome to prepare the way: John Ireland (first archbishop of St. Paul) and Bishop John Keane of Richmond. When he arrived toward the end of 1887 he learned that they had had little success. Gibbons made his own calls on members of the Congregation of the Holy Office and was met with silence. At last indignant, he told the secretary of the congregation that he would hold the Holy Office responsible for the loss of souls in the United States. Only then did he get a promise that the matter would be restudied.

The cardinal decided to make his case on paper. He wrote a long document outlining the goals of labor, responding to every objection he could imagine being raised, stressing the consequences to the Church if the condemnation was applied in the United States. It was a masterful piece of work — frank, sincere, convincing. It accomplished its purpose. Bishop Keane wrote to Cardinal Henry Manning in England, who was supporting Gibbons, that the American cardinal finally met with the top officials of the Holy Office and that the outcome of the meeting was "that the Bishops of America are the safest guide of the Holy Office in its action on American affairs and they will let well enough alone."

The struggle in Rome did not escape notice in the United States. A reporter from the New York *Herald* managed to obtain a copy of the document Gibbons had submitted to the Holy Office. His story of Gibbons's defense of labor made headlines across the United States, Canada, and Europe. Editorial comment was on the whole strongly favorable to the cardinal, although there were some dissenting voices. *The Nation* observed that the United States suffered a terrible loss to politics when Gibbons entered the priesthood. The New York *Times* was critical, observing "that the Church will make a terrible blunder if it permits him to persuade it into taking sides of an organization which is trying to substitute brute force and intimidation for law, reason, equity and precepts of the Christian religion." The paper went on to accuse the cardinal of weak judgment and cynicism. The affair came to an end when the Holy See issued its formal finding and ruled that the Knights of Labor "could be tolerated." The final vindication came when Leo XIII issued his famed encyclical *Rerum Novarum* (Of New Things), which put the Church squarely on the side of labor.

Cardinal Gibbons's return to Baltimore after receiving the red hat was a triumph. A parade had been arranged from Union Station to the cardinal's residence on Charles Street. Over one hundred thousand Baltimoreans lined the streets and some eight thousand marched in the parade. All the civic officials were on hand to welcome "Our Cardinal" home. Workingmen cheered for the defense he made of their rights. Catholics did not hide their pride at having a cardinal of their own. Even Protestants approved of the great honor that had come to Baltimore. There was no question but that Cardinal James Gibbons had a firm hold on the hearts of the people among whom he lived.

However, a new controversy was brewing that would require all the cardinal's skills. It was a controversy which

involved the relationship between Church and State. The mindset of the Vatican was that of a close alliance between Church and State, indeed, an identification of the two. It was rooted in the ideal days when the Papal States were surrounded by Catholic kingdoms whose rulers would come barefoot in the snow seeking pardon from the pope for some wrong they had committed. But those days were gone. Catholic kings had disappeared and the Enlightenment had labeled the Church its enemy. France, the "eldest daughter" of the Church, was a child in rebellion. In Italy the pope was the "prisoner of the Vatican," and radicals had even assaulted the corpse of his predecessor, Pius IX. Elsewhere in Europe the Protestant Reformation had long since done its work. Despite prevailing conditions, the Vatican curia longed for what no longer was possible and did not understand the American ideal of separation of Church and State. When Rome wanted to begin a hierarchy in the United States, it made its request to Benjamin Franklin, ambassador to France during the American Revolution, through its papal nuncio in Paris. Franklin forwarded the request to the American Congress which advised him to tell the nuncio that because of the nature of the application — being purely spiritual — Congress had no power to either reject it or approve it. When the reply reached Rome that the Church was free to do as it pleased without political interference, it seemed almost naïve because for many centuries the Church had been getting approval from Catholic governments on individuals it could or could not appoint.

Gibbons, a keen student of history, once remarked that the greatest enemies of the Church were the so-called Christian kings and that only in the United States did

Catholics find themselves truly at home. On his return from one European trip he remarked, "The oftener I go to Europe, the more gratified I am to be an American citizen." When Gibbons was installed in the Roman church that was put in his care, his address on that occasion was a sterling defense of the American system of government which left religion free to develop as it would. Regarding this sermon, the Paulist founder, Isaac Hecker, observed that it took courage for Gibbons to do what he did in the center of Christendom, adding, "He has been able to express the American idea in such terms as not to be misunderstood."

But there were many in Rome who did not want to understand. They rejected the "Americanizers" out of hand and let it be known that they suspected strong Protestant influences. There were whispers of heresy and talk behind the backs of American prelates when they visited Rome. Some attributed this to jealousy, but ignorance was nearer to the truth. The Italians of the curia simply did not understand the United States and the American way of doing things. The matter came to a head with the publication of a book, and the American heresy was born and required official action of the Church. The book was Father Walter Elliott's *Life of Father Isaac Thomas Hecker*. Father Elliott, also a Paulist, had written the biography simply to recount the life of an important American churchman while it was still fresh in the minds of contemporaries. Father Hecker, an unusual and outstanding man, had been closely allied with many leading American figures, had given missions and lectured widely across the United States, and was well known. Archbishop Ireland contributed the introduction to the book in which he called Hecker "the flower of our American priesthood." It was a type of book that had been published before and often since; but now it would lead to the American heresy or — as one biographer of Gibbons calls it — "The Phantom Heresy." This is not quite accurate. While the heresy did not exist in the United States, it did find roots in Europe.

The heresy came about when a French edition of Father Hecker's life was published. A book which had sold relatively few copies in America suddenly became popular in France. Liberals and radicals exaggerated its contents and developed from it new teachings called Americanism which gave preference to the laity over bishops, activism over contemplation, and doctrinal compromise over orthodoxy in order to reach accommodation with non-Catholics. Neither Father Hecker in particular nor American Catholics in general ever promoted such principles; but French conservatives, foes of the liberals, implied that they did and they cried out for condemnation. The controversy spread beyond France; German Jesuits took up the cudgels against Americanism and there were cries to put *The Life of Father Isaac Thomas Hecker* on the Index of Forbidden Books (a list, incidentally, which is no longer in force).

Cardinal Gibbons could have sidestepped the issue, but he did not. He wrote a preface to a new edition of the life in which he lauded Hecker as a model priest. This led to attacks on the cardinal himself which accused him of conspiring to become pope, of promoting Protestantism and Freemasonry, and calling for him to be censured by the pope. Gibbons ignored the personal attacks but could not overlook the accusations against the American Church.

He wrote a strongly worded defense to the Holy See in which he argued the term "Americanism" was being used as a "scarecrow" to suggest something erroneous and heretical. He concluded by stating, "I have no hesitation in affirming that you have not in the whole world an episcopate, a clergy, and believers more fundamentally Catholic, firmer in their faith, and more wholly devoted to the Holy See."

The Gibbons letter arrived at a crucial moment. The Holy Office had prepared a decree of condemnation for the Hecker book and sent it to the pope for his signature. The choice was now up to the pope. He refused to sign the decree, saying he was reserving the matter to himself. The result was the apostolic letter *Testem Benevolentiae* (Proof of Our Love), issued January 22, 1899, and addressed to "Our Beloved Son, James Cardinal Gibbons." The papal response condemned those things which had been put forth under the name of Americanism and found fault with some of the spirituality in the Hecker book; but nowhere did it condemn the book, the American bishops, or the American Church. Nevertheless, some bishops interpreted an implied criticism and Archbishop Ireland was especially irate. Cardinal Gibbons was more serene: "It has no application in our own country, but I suppose the Holy Father had to act."

As the pope's letter was addressed to him, the cardinal felt he had to reply. He let the dust settle and then in mid-March wrote to Leo XIII and thanked him for casting "light on these questions." He said that the doctrine called Americanism was extravagant and absurd with nothing in common to Americans themselves, adding, "I do not think that there can be found in the entire country, a bishop, a priest, or even a layman with a knowledge of his religion who has ever uttered such enormities. No, this is not — it never has been and never will be — our Americanism. I am deeply grateful to Your Holiness for having yourself made this distinction in your apostolic letter." Archbishop Ireland wanted to go further. At the annual meeting of archbishops he proposed all bishops be polled on the matter. When the vote was a tie, Gibbons who chaired these meetings broke the tie by voting "no." He wanted to put the matter to rest. Some time later Leo replied that while the tendencies in many nations cause sorrow for the Holy See, the condition of the Church in America "cheers Our heart and fills it with delight." Thus the matter finally ended.

It was also one of the final acts of the pope. The ninety-three-year old pontiff had begun to fail. Gibbons had love and admiration for Leo, and news that he was dying filled him with great sadness. But he was also practical. No American had ever taken part in a papal election and he resolved to be the first. Church law allowed ten days for the election of a pope. Cardinal John McCloskey of New York, the first American cardinal, had tried to get to Rome for the election of Leo XIII and had failed. Cardinal Gibbons made reservations on ship after ship, canceling each to make the next. Early in July he received word from Rome that Leo was close to death. He left at once for the Vatican and had reached Paris when he learned the news of the pope's passing. The conclave provided a lesson that made him appreciate even more his American heritage. The leading candidate for the papacy was Cardinal Mariano Rampolla del Tindaro who received the majority of votes on the first ballot. Gibbons knew Rampolla well, having dealt with the Vatican secretary of state on many issues, and he assured him that he would receive the necessary two thirds on the next ballot or two. Just then the cardinal from Cracow announced that Emperor Francis Joseph I of Austria was using his veto against Rampolla. Gibbons was shocked at this political interference; but he knew Austria, France, and Spain could veto any candidate. Once again he was grateful for American separation of Church and State. The conclave finally settled on Cardinal Giuseppe Sarto from Venice, who assumed the name Pius X, one of the great popes of modern times (1903-1914).

So the years passed. On June 6, 1911, Baltimore held a civic ceremony to honor the seventy-seven-year-old Cardinal Gibbons, who on that day was celebrating the fiftieth anniversary of his priesthood and twenty-fifth as a cardinal. The festivities were held in the Baltimore Armory, and on the platform was President William H. Taft; former President Theodore Roosevelt; Champ Clark, Speaker of the House; Chief Justice Edward White; the governor of Maryland; Baltimore's mayor; the Protestant Episcopal bishop of Maryland; and other dignitaries. The Washington *Post* reported: "The business of the U.S. Government, superficially at least, was at a standstill yesterday, owing to the exodus of public men to attend the anniversary ceremonies. Assistant Secretaries held down the lid of most government departments, most of the cabinet officers going to Baltimore on the President's special train." Speech after speech was made extolling the cardinal and although the ceremony took four hours, he was the last to leave the platform, accepting the greetings of Catholics, Protestants, and Jews, all of whom held the old

203

man in love and respect. The *Post* summed it up in a bit of hyperbole: "Such a demonstration was never before seen on this hemisphere."

Cardinal Gibbons had ten years more to live and things to do, so if the celebration in Baltimore was meant as a last hurrah, the cardinal would still outlive many of its participants. Within weeks of the double jubilee, he received word from Rome of the approval of the Catholic Foreign Mission Society (Maryknoll) which he had proposed to the American archbishops and then sent its founders to the Vatican for approval. In October there was a Church celebration of the double jubilee at the Catholic University in Washington, during which Archbishop John Farley of New York called him "the most beloved man in the Catholic Church in America." The following year Gibbons delivered the invocation at the Democratic Convention that nominated Woodrow Wilson. The year after that he was in Rome for the installation of a new pope, Benedict XV, despite the fact that World War I was on and the Atlantic was unsafe. When President Woodrow Wilson went to Europe for the peace conference, Cardinal Gibbons recommended that he see the pope, which the president did. The cardinal lost two causes, having supported the president's League of Nations and opposed the prohibition act (which made it illegal to make, transport, and sell alcoholic beverages). Congress killed League membership and voted in prohibition (which was in effect from 1920 to 1933).

So 1921 arrived. Old age and failing health kept Cardinal Gibbons confined to his house on Charles Street in Baltimore. There were occasional rides about the city in a car and a few visitors received in his home. As Holy Week approached, his heart was growing weaker and weaker. On Palm Sunday he had another attack. The apostolic delegate called to give the cardinal the papal blessing and the cardinal told him that the end was near. On Tuesday he received Holy Communion for the last time. The next day he told a young priest who was attending him, "My boy, I shall die tomorrow." On March 24, he kept his word, for at 11:33 A.M. of Holy Thursday, 1921, the man who had become "Our Cardinal" for all Catholic America breathed his last. The mayor of Baltimore ordered the bells of city hall to be tolled eighty-six times — James Gibbons would have been eighty-seven years old in July of that year — and thus the people of his beloved city learned that their cardinal was with them no more.

# PART FIVE

## The Women □ *INTRODUCTION*

Historians have not paid great heed to the contribution that women have made to the building of Catholic America for the simple reason that what is unknown remains unsung. There are women who turn up in historical accounts, four of whom will be eulogized in the following pages. There are others who could have been as easily mentioned: Mother Catherine Spalding, who did so much for frontier life; Mother Katharine Drexel, who deserted Philadelphia's Main Line for Indian missions; activists like Bella Dodd and Martha Moore Avery, both converted Marxists; Rose Hawthorne Lathrop, the convert-daughter of Nathaniel Hawthorne, who devoted her life to the incurable sick. But beyond are the untold numbers of Sisters who belonged to such communities as the Sisters of Loretto and the Sisters of Charity of Nazareth — and so many others who brought education and civilization to the American frontier as it moved West. Among these unsung builders of Catholic America are Sisters from Europe who came with the immigrants in order to preserve their faith. Others include American communities which came into existence to fill specific needs of the emerging nation.

Particularly to be mentioned are those pioneer women — wives and mothers — who moved West with their men and at a given moment could have in their hands a gun or a plow. It was these women who built the homes, who aided priests to settle among them, who demanded education for their children and insisted on law and order. All-male camps were wild and riotous places. It was not until women came that civilization also arrived. Men pioneered trails, but women turned those trails into roadways and then village streets. While men may stalk the pages of our history books, behind every page is an army of women to whom American civilization really belongs. Every family can boast of these women who had no confusion as to their identities as mothers and builders of America.

# CHAPTER 13

## The Bridge

### *Elizabeth Ann Seton*

Elizabeth Ann Bayley Seton was born on August 28, 1774, in the city of New York, a week before the First Continental Congress met in Philadelphia; thus, while a child of a British colony, she grew up in the infant days of the new American republic. She carried the genes of French, Dutch, and English ancestors. By blood or marriage she was related to American high society of her day — the Barclays, Roosevelts, De Lanceys, Whites, Van Cortlandts, and Pells. A great-great-grandfather had been a Huguenot; but she was baptized in the Episcopal Church and, as a widow, became a Catholic. She was, then, a bridge between the old and the new, the rich and the poor, Protestants and Catholics, the married and unmarried.

Elizabeth's father, Richard, was a prominent physician. He served with the British Army during the American Revolution and later taught medicine at what is now Columbia University. Her mother, Catherine, died in 1777. Left with three small daughters, her father soon remarried. Her father sent Elizabeth to a private school and saw to it that she was well educated. Her childhood and youth were not completely happy years. She spent considerable time with relatives, since her stepmother had little interest in her, preferring her own children over those she inherited, and her father was of little help. This was most clearly shown by her father's will which left everything to his new wife and her heirs, and nothing to his daughters by his first wife. Her stepmother's will in turn divided her husband's estate among her natural children and did not mention her stepdaughters who thus by both wills were left penniless. Elizabeth provided for her own security when in 1794 at the age of nineteen she married William Magee Seton, six years older than herself. It was not a marriage of convenience, however, but one of love.

William Seton, who joined his father in his shipping business, came from a prominent family of Scotch lineage. The years were affluent, and five children came from the marriage of William Seton and Elizabeth Ann Bayley: three girls and two boys. The only cloud on the horizon was William's none-too-robust health which showed itself in a cough and a "pain in the breast." Elizabeth devoted herself to her husband, her children, and her many charities. All seemed serene. Then a series of tragedies struck. The elder Seton died suddenly and William had to take over the business. The French raided his merchantmen and there were business failures in London and Hamburg. By autumn of 1799 the Seton firm was in bankruptcy. Elizabeth's father caught fever, perhaps cholera, from immigrants entering New York, and he died. William's tuberculosis became virulent and in desperation he proposed that they go to Leghorn, Italy, where he had friends — the Filicchi family — and hope that the climate there would help him. So Elizabeth parceled out four of her children among relatives and with her husband and oldest child, Anna, set sail for Italy in the fall of 1803.

New troubles awaited them. When they reached Leghorn, the Italian immigration officials, aware that there had been an outbreak of yellow fever in New York, told the ill Seton that he would have to be quarantined; so he was carried off the ship to the Italian lazaretto and held there for a month. He was released on December 20 and carried to the home of Antonio Filicchi where Elizabeth and Anna had found hospitality. William managed to last through Christmas; he died on December 27 and was buried in the Protestant cemetery of Leghorn. Through all this trying period, Elizabeth found great consolation in the Filicchis. This family was the first Catholic family she knew, and she was edified that they lived the religion they professed. She and Anna attended Mass and went on pilgrimages with the Filicchis until the two found passage back to New York in February. The Italian experience was a turning point in the life of Elizabeth Seton. Two Catholic doctrines — the Real Presence and the Motherhood of Mary — had particular fascination for her, and it seemed as if she was given faith without asking for it. The Filicchis had given her books to read; but she was not yet ready to take the final step, although her daughter Anna asked her, "Ma, won't we go to the Catholic Church when we get home?"

Back in New York, Elizabeth had to depend on the charity of friends. They helped her to get a small house where she lived on the second floor and rented out the first. She struggled with the matter of conversion. New York in those days was a bigoted place. Episcopalianism was the unofficial state religion, and its adherents looked down on Protestants belonging to what were considered lesser sects. As for Roman Catholics, all that they could attract — in the Episcopalians' view — were "ignorant Irish immigrants," good only for menial tasks. Often, Elizabeth passed the only Catholic church in town — St.

Peter's on Barclay Street; but she did not dare enter because she knew that to do so would mean ostracism for herself and her children. On Ash Wednesday of 1805 she finally did go in and two weeks later formally submitted herself to the Church in the presence of Father Matthew O'Brien, professing to believe what the Council of Trent taught. A week later she made her first confession and a week after that her first Holy Communion, recording in a letter, "GOD IS MINE AND I AM HIS! . . . I have received Him."

Elizabeth's conversion was not without cost and she found herself estranged from most of her family and friends, although there were some who while not agreeing with her recognized her right to choose her way of life. To support herself she went into a partnership with a man and his wife to open a school, but her partners were poor business people and the school failed. A relative suggested a boarding school for children without mothers and this she began with a dozen children. About this time Bishop John Carroll came to New York and the two met, each impressed with the other. The bishop gave her a week's instruction and confirmed her. She needed the strength the sacrament would give her because her sister-in-law Cecilia Seton, moved by Elizabeth's example, asked to be received into the Church too. This "treachery" brought a storm of protest and persecution from the vast Seton clan. Cecilia had to leave her home and move in with Elizabeth, and the conversion played a role in the riots that broke out before St. Peter's Church. The bigotry the conversion created also affected her boarding school, and children were withdrawn. Affairs had now come to a crisis point.

There were few people to whom Elizabeth could talk. Educated and cultivated Catholics were rare, particularly in New York, so it is not surprising that Elizabeth turned to priests, particularly those from France, and carried on a lively correspondence. She wrote frequent letters to John Cheverus, who was to become the first bishop of Boston; Francis Matignon, a Boston pastor; Louis William Dubourg, rector of St. Mary's Seminary in Baltimore; and Father John Tisserant, a New Jersey pastor who served as her spiritual director. It was through this correspondence that her move to Maryland finally came. She was concerned about the education of her boys. Father Dubourg recommended Montreal; but in discussing the matter with Father Cheverus and others, it was decided that Georgetown would be more appropriate. So it was arranged: Mrs. Seton would go to Baltimore and open a Catholic school, and her sons would enter Georgetown. Thus on June 8, 1808, Elizabeth Seton and her children sailed out of New York harbor aboard the *Grand Sachem* for Baltimore, arriving there on the feast of Corpus Christi. She went directly to St. Mary's, where a new chapel was being dedicated. The pontifical Mass with its music overwhelmed her. She wrote to Cecilia: "Human nature could scarcely bear it — your imagination could never conceive the splendor, the glory of the scene." After Mass she was welcomed by Bishop Carroll, Father Dubourg, and the many Catholic laity at the ceremony. For the first time she felt at home in the Church.

A house — which would also serve as the school — had been prepared for the family on Paca Street. Elizabeth found a new spiritual director, Father Pierre Babade, with whom she had immediate rapport. That fall her boys went to Georgetown, and Elizabeth began her school with seven pupils (her three girls and four boarders), adding three more boarders before Christmas. Father Dubourg and his friends had another hope for Paca Street — that a religious community of women would develop from it. Although Sisters had come to Canada in the early days of French settlement, there were none in the United States. The French priests knew what women could contribute to the Church's development. Whether they had discussed this with Elizabeth before the move to Baltimore is not clear; but a month after her arrival Elizabeth was writing to the Filicchis about the school, saying it was her hope "that there will not be wanting ladies to join in forming a permanent institution." A short time later she wrote a friend and called herself "your poor little Nun." Meanwhile, a young lady from Philadelphia, Cecilia Conway, joined the house on Paca Street. She had been planning on going to Spain to join a convent, but Father Babade persuaded her to join Elizabeth.

On March 25, 1809, Elizabeth pronounced the vows of poverty, chastity, and obedience, binding for one year, and became known as Mother Seton. Other young ladies came to join the group, and — on June 1 — Elizabeth and four of her spiritual daughters donned the religious habit for the first time. Cecilia Seton, her health very fragile, joined the group. Paca Street was overcrowded. The Sulpicians had begun a foundation fifty miles to the northwest, at Emmitsburg, on the Pennsylvania border. They suggested that Mother Seton move her community there; moreover, the mountain air would be good for Cecilia Seton's health. So on June 21, in a Conestoga wagon, the trek to the Catoctin Mountains was begun; the travelers arrived four days later at St. Mary's College where Father John Dubois was awaiting them.

214

At Emmitsburg, the little community (calling itself the Sisters of Charity) began to grow and soon there were twenty members. They followed the rule of St. Vincent de Paul, and the garb Mother Seton selected was contemporary — the black dress and small bonnet of the Italian widow. In October, John Carroll, now an archbishop, made his first visit and was pleased with the development of the first community of nuns in the United States. More postulants came and a new building was erected. It was at Emmitsburg that Mother Seton was to meet Father Simon Bruté who would not only become a friend for life but who would guide her through the spiritual life to sanctity. The rules and constitutions of the new community were ratified in 1812 and although the Sisters were developing strongly, personal tragedy was still with Mother Seton. Her own health was not good — she suffered constrictions of the chest. Cecilia Seton died, and then Mother Seton's daughter Anna fell ill and died on March 12, 1812. Anna had been received into the community shortly before her death. In 1814 the first foundation was made outside Maryland when the Sisters were put in charge of an orphanage in Philadelphia. Three years later Mother Seton was to send three nuns to New York to begin work there.

Mother Seton's last years were not easy ones. In 1816 her daughter Rebecca became the second of her children to die. Rebecca had imitated the sanctity of her mother and as she lay deathly ill told Mother Seton, "I know the happiness of an early death, and to sin no more." On the afternoon of November 2 (she was to die the next day) she said to those around her, "I have just handed Our Lord my little cup. It is quite full. He will come for me." Thus Rebecca joined her sister Anna in the little cemetery of the motherhouse. Mother Seton was not as fortunate with her two boys, each of whom was self-centered and trying to her heart. So the years passed and Mother Seton grew more and more frail. The end came for her on January 4, 1821. She was only forty-seven years old. Tuberculosis was the probable cause of her death.

Father Simon Bruté sent the news to Antonio Filicchi: "We deposited her precious remains on the day following that of her death. In this little wood she reposes with about fifteen Sisters and novices who had come to join her. She leaves more than fifty Sisters to survive her, to regret her [passing] and to follow in her footsteps — forty of them at St. Joseph's, the others at the Mountain, in Philadelphia and New York. . . . How profound her faith and how tender her piety! How sincere her humility, combined with so great intelligence! How great her goodness and kindness to all!"

The movement Mother Seton began was to grow and expand after her death, reaching even beyond the borders of the United States. The schools, colleges, and hospitals her Sisters founded would make Christ's charity present across the United States. In an age when the American nation was beginning to grow and the Catholic Church was struggling to find its place in the new country, Mother Seton brought the touch and love of a mother, and the story of our nation would be incomplete without citing her contribution.

Elizabeth Ann Bayley Seton became the first native-born American to be named a saint when Pope Paul VI canonized her on September 14, 1975.

# CHAPTER 14

## *Sanctity on the Frontier*

### *Rose Philippine Duchesne*

When Mother Rose Philippine Duchesne died in St. Charles, Missouri, in 1852, Father Pierre Jean De Smet, the celebrated missioner to the Indians, wrote her religious Sisters, urging them to publish a biography. "No greater saint," he said, "ever died in Missouri, or perhaps in the whole Union." The Church agreed with Father De Smet because in 1940 this valiant woman was given the title of "Blessed" and declared worthy of veneration and imitation.

Rose Philippine Duchesne was born into a prosperous merchant family of Grenoble, France, in 1769. Since she was born on the eve of the feast of St. Rose of Lima, first saint of the New World, she was given that saint's name. Among the visitors who came to her parents' home when she was a child was a Jesuit missioner from Louisiana whose stories about Indians were to become a motivation in her future life. The young girl was educated by tutors and went to a school directed by Visitation Sisters. When she was seventeen and her family was seeking a suitable husband for her, she announced that she was joining the nuns who were teaching her. At first the family objected but later relented when she stood firm. However, when she was preparing to make her first profession a year and a half later, her father forbade it because of the uncertainty of the times. His foreboding was realized when the French Revolution resulted in the expulsion of many religious communities, including the Visitation Sisters — and Rose was forced to return home.

In the years that followed she tried to live as a religious: tending the sick, visiting those in prison, and educating the young. When Napoleon ended the persecution of the Church and signed a concordat with the Holy See in 1801, Rose bought the buildings of her old convent and sought to restore a Visitation presence, but her effort failed. Hearing of a new group of Sisters that was starting, Society of the Sacred Heart, she approached the founder, the future St. Madeleine Sophie Barat, and offered her the buildings she had bought; thus, at the age of thirty-three, Rose Philippine Duchesne became a postulant in the new community. In 1806 a Cistercian abbot who had sent the first Trappists to North America visited her convent and spoke about the missions across the Atlantic. The visit reawakened her missionary ardor and she spoke to Mother Barat about sending her to the missions. While Mother Barat approved in principle, she told her zealous friend that the new community would have to have firm footing at home before venturing overseas.

Rose Duchesne was forty-nine years of age when the order finally came to her. Mother Barat had been visited by Bishop Louis William Dubourg of St. Louis who asked for some of her religious when they could be spared. The matter might have been put off indefinitely except for gentle reminders from Mother Duchesne, until at last in March 1818 Mother Duchesne led a band of four other religious to a ship at Bordeaux and set sail for the New World. The journey in those days was not easy. They spent eleven weeks at sea before New Orleans was reached. "Seasickness is really evil," Mother Duchesne wrote back. "It affects the head as well as the stomach and makes one useless for anything." But the journey was not over at New Orleans; ahead lay forty-seven days up the Mississippi to St. Louis, which they reached on what Mother Duchesne thought was a propitious day — May 29, feast of the Sacred Heart — only to learn that she and her companions were unexpected and that there was no work for them among the Indians!

Bishop Dubourg finally decided to send them to St. Charles, Missouri, where there were French, Creole, and English Catholics, poor and in need. He found them a log cabin in which to live and there on the frontier these refined French women opened the first free school west of the Mississippi. A year later a new foundation was begun at Florissant — a convent, a boarding school, and a novitiate when the first American girl, Mary Layton, joined the new community. Still later, an orphanage, academy, and free school were begun in St. Louis. In time she would found six houses of her society from New Orleans to St. Louis, making frequent and lengthy trips on the mighty river. On one journey yellow fever broke out on the boat and she nursed the sick, baptizing one man before he died. Through her ministrations she caught the disease herself and she was put ashore at Natchez to die. She survived, as she was to survive other tribulations and trials which came her way and that of her Sisters. She was able to share some of her burdens with the Jesuits when they arrived in St. Louis in 1823; but as one Jesuit wrote, "It is difficult to tell whether in the ensuing period the Society of the Sacred Heart owed more to the Society of Jesus or the Fathers to the nuns." Bishop Dubourg had moved his headquarters to New Orleans, so the Jesuits became the ones Mother Duchesne relied upon for advice and assistance.

Mother Duchesne and her nuns brought a gentility to the American frontier. They provided education for poor children who otherwise would never have had any. They trained girls not only to become wives and mothers but to be ladies. The contributions they made to those living in the Mississippi Valley have never been truly assayed, but they were great. Even though she was a woman of indomitable spirit with great trust in God's providence, the years had fatigued Mother Duchesne. When she was seventy-one years old, however, she got the opportunity to realize her dream of working exclusively among the Indians. It happened this way: In 1840 an assistant of Mother Barat came from France to inspect the Mississippi foundations. Mother Duchesne asked to resign as American superior and her request was granted. At the same time Father De Smet was asking the assistant general for some nuns to open a school among the Potawatomis at Sugar Creek in present-day Kansas. Mother Duchesne asked to be included in the contingent of four nuns to be assigned there. She was told that she could go "if you are able to travel."

Thus a dream that began with a girl of eight in Grenoble, France, was finally realized by an old woman in an Indian village in what was to be the state of Kansas; but dreams do not always turn out as expected. Mother Duchesne was too old to learn the Potawatomi language, so she spoke the international language of kindness and love. Since she could not teach, she decided to pray for the success of their work. She spent four hours in the morning and four hours in the evening lost in prayer in the simple chapel. The Indians named her "Woman Who Always Prays." One young Indian, who found it difficult to believe that Mother Duchesne could remain kneeling for long periods of time in profound prayer, one day crept into the chapel and arranged corn kernels on the skirt of her habit. When the Indian youth returned hours later, Mother Duchesne was still absorbed in prayer, and the kernels of corn remained exactly as he had placed them. Mother Duchesne's new dream was to go to the Indians of the Rocky Mountains, but it was not to be. Her health began to fail and she was recalled to Missouri. "I do not know the reason for this recall," she said, "but God knows and that is enough."

Her last years were spent at St. Charles, where despite ill health she continued her long prayers and mortifications. One Sister who knew her well wrote: "She was the St. Francis of Assisi of the Society. Everything in and about her was stamped with the seal of a crucified life. She would have liked to disappear from the sight of men, and may it be said no one occupied less space in this world than Madame Duchesne. Her room was a miserable hole with a single window, in which paper supplied the place of some of the panes; her bed was a mattress two inches thick, laid on the ground by night and put away in the day in the cupboard; her only covering at night was an old piece of black stuff with a cross like a pall."

Thus on November 18, 1852, at the age of eighty-three, Mother Duchesne's missionary life ended. The work she founded grew from a one-room log school in St. Charles, Missouri, to colleges extending from New York to California — and the religious of the province she founded have carried her spirit to South America and

Australia. The feast day of this valiant woman is observed on November 17. This builder of Catholic America wrote home in her early days in Missouri of her poverty and difficulties. Her brother immediately replied that he would send her the money for passage back to France. "Use the money to pay the passage of two more nuns coming to America!" she replied, revealing the stuff of which our Catholic pioneers were made.

# CHAPTER 15

## Citizen Saint

### *Frances Xavier Cabrini*

The first person in the United States to be named a saint was not born in America but came to this country from Europe, specifically Italy. Perhaps this was fitting; for while Catholic roots in America go back to colonial days, Catholics were a tiny minority in an Anglo-Saxon Protestant culture. It was not until the waves of European immigrants began reaching our shores that Catholics became a force in the life of the United States. The vitality that they brought to their new homeland is aptly commemorated in one of their number, a naturalized citizen who became our first canonized saint. She was Mother Frances Xavier Cabrini.

Mother Cabrini was born in Lombardy, Italy, the thirteenth child of Agostino and Stella Cabrini, on July 15, 1850. Nine of the Cabrini children died before getting out of their teens. The Cabrinis' last child was so tiny and frail that she was immediately carried to the parish church where she was baptized Francesca Maria, names of two deceased sisters. But the new baby was not to die in infancy. Although small for her age and never seemingly robust, she grew up with a tenacity of will that belied her size and was a tribute to her peasant origins. As a child she confided that she wanted to be a missionary Sister and she was assiduous in her studies so that she might acquire knowledge she could pass on to others. For her secondary studies she was sent to a school run by the Daughters of the Sacred Heart. Here she excelled in languages — Latin, French, and Italian; she also did well in mathematics, science, and history, the latter being her favorite subject. She passed with high grades and was awarded a license to teach school.

A secular career, however, was not Francesca's desire. She had her heart set on becoming a religious and a missioner. She applied to join the Daughters of the Sacred Heart, but these Sisters who knew and respected her turned her down because they did not think she was physically strong enough. In a way it was providential, for the year 1869 was to be a year of tragic blows. First, her beloved father died, then her mother, next an uncle (a retired priest who lived with them), and finally her sister Maddalena who had been crippled from childhood with polio. She nursed each of them up until the end, and when time could be found she cared for other sick in her village. With her parents gone, she relied for advice and direction on her pastor, Don Antonio Serrati, for whom she also taught school. She applied again to the Daughters of the Sacred Heart and to the Canossian Sisters without success.

Francesca's entrance into the religious life came almost accidentally. Don Serrati had been transferred to Codogno where along with his parish he inherited an orphanage, or rather a group of orphans who were kept through parish funds by a local woman who maintained the girls in disgraceful conditions. Desperate to remedy things, Monsignor Serrati asked Francesca if she could come to Codogno and help him. She came and for three years worked under conditions others would call intolerable, opposed at every step by the woman who owned the houses. Her consolation was in the orphans. One day seven of them came to her and told her that since Francesca frequently said she wanted to be a missioner, they wanted to be missioners with her. Francesca cultivated these seven and finally went to Monsignor Serrati and told him they wanted to consecrate themselves to God by means of vows. He consented and she took the name of St. Francis Xavier, the great Jesuit missioner, and henceforth would be known as Mother Frances Xavier Cabrini. She convinced the pastor that the orphans could not continue under present conditions. In a meeting with the bishop of the diocese it was decided to transfer the orphans to private homes. The question then became one of what to do with Mother Cabrini and her seven Sisters.

"Monsignor Serrati has told me you have always dreamed of becoming a missioner," the bishop told her, "but there is no missionary institute around here. Why not begin one yourself?"

Matters moved swiftly. She found an old monastery that had been suppressed by Napoleon. Monsignor Serrati arranged for its purchase and Mother Cabrini persuaded the bishop to allow her to take the orphan girls there instead of scattering them. He agreed, and on the afternoon of November 12, 1880, Mother Cabrini, her seven Sisters, and a group of excited orphan girls followed three donkey carts loaded with bedding, cooking utensils, and food supplies to their new home. Thus did the Missionary Sisters of the Sacred Heart begin. The days that followed were busy ones for the frail nun. She had to put the new house in order, find furnishings, arrange schedules and schooling, recruit new Sisters, and raise the finances to keep everything going. Within a year the old monastery had to be enlarged, and soon requests were coming from other parishes and dioceses for personnel and new foundations.

One night she had a dream in which Jesus appeared to her as a child. "Go to Rome," the Boy Jesus told her. She arrived in Rome on September 24, 1887, penniless, without friends or means to reach those in high places. She and a companion, Sister Serafina, found shelter with some Franciscan Sisters, and she learned that the person she should see was Cardinal Parocchi. It took her three days to get an appointment, and when she finally met with the cardinal, he told her he had never heard of her or her community. Going to the foreign missions was quite out of the question; she had no history behind her community and no money. The cardinal suggested that she return to Codogno. Since the cardinal had only "suggested," Mother Cabrini reasoned, she decided to remain in Rome, writing letters, calling on whoever would see her, and encountering discouragement after discouragement stoically. She continued to call on Cardinal Parocchi, who was becoming more and more impressed with her abilities and perseverance. Finally, after a month, the cardinal proposed that she open a free school in Rome and a nursery in the suburbs. It was all she needed. She sent a message to Codogno: "Pick out five Sisters, fill suitcases with linen and kitchen utensils, raise money for their train fare, and send them to me." She rented an apartment on Via Nomentana for her headquarters and begged the needed furnishings.

Rome soon came to know this indefatigable nun, and within a year she had received from the Holy See the

"Decretum Laudis" (the official approval of her institute). She made new foundations, but the foreign missions were always uppermost in her mind. A new friend, Bishop Giovanni Scalabrini of Piacenza, spoke to her of the needs of Italian immigrants in America; she was not, however, thinking of America but of the Orient. On another occasion, he told her that he had spoken with Archbishop Michael Corrigan of New York who would welcome her there. But she could not decide.

The answer came in her long-awaited audience with Pope Leo XIII. After preliminary conversation about her family, her background, and her institute, the pope went directly to what he had probably been briefed on by Cardinal Parocchi and Bishop Scalabrini. He spoke to her of the growing importance of the United States, the contributions that immigrant Italians could make there, and of their spiritual needs. "Your field awaits you not in the East but the West," the pope said. "Go to America!" One did not refuse the pope, so on March 23, 1889, Mother Cabrini and six of her Sisters (seven among thirteen hundred passengers) sailed from Le Havre. They began their new work by tending to the needs of the nine hundred immigrants in steerage. On March 31 the Sisters saw the welcoming torch of the Statue of Liberty.

Mother Cabrini was surprised that there was no representative of Archbishop Corrigan or the Scalabrini Fathers to meet the new arrivals. The group made its way out of the confusion and at dusk arrived at the Scalabrini parish on the lower east side. Here they learned that they were not expected. The Fathers rented some rooms for them for the night until they could see the archbishop the next day. After attending Mass the next morning in the

parish, they went to Archbishop Corrigan. He too was surprised by their presence. He told Mother Cabrini that the orphanage he had been planning had fallen through. He had written this in a letter to Bishop Scalabrini, but somehow his message must have not reached the Sisters. It would be best for Mother and her Sisters to return to Italy, he added.

"That cannot be," Mother Cabrini told the archbishop. "I received my orders from Peter's Chair. America is the mission to which I have been assigned. Here we must stay."

The archbishop knew when he had met his match. He arranged for Mother Cabrini and her Sisters to stay with the Irish Sisters of Charity on Madison Avenue. He told them to open a school for Italian children in the Scalabrini parish and do whatever they could to help the immigrants. It was no easy challenge. The Italian immigrants were the poorest of the poor; illiterate and uneducated, they were exploited by politicians, landlords, merchants, and employers. Urgent problems abounded on every side. The Missionary Sisters of the Sacred Heart were soon familiar figures on Mott and Mulberry Streets and in their fetid tenements into which the immigrants were crowded. Human misery and human problems were everywhere. Mother Cabrini learned that the Countess Cesnola (née Mary Reid) had offered five thousand dollars for the orphanage but that the archbishop had done nothing because, while the money would buy a building, he did not have the means to feed the orphans, pay the utility bills, and keep the project going. On Palm Sunday Mother Cabrini and the countess saw the archbishop, and on April 21 Mother Cabrini led her Sisters to their new home on Fifty-ninth Street — the countess's money had bought the building, her friends had helped furnish it, and the Missionary Sisters of the Sacred Heart had their first American foundation. Begging had gotten them started and begging was to keep them going. Mother Cabrini soon realized that the archbishop was right and that Fifty-ninth Street was no place for an orphanage; so with the help of the archbishop a religious house at West Park — north of the city on the Hudson River — was transferred to her and here the orphanage was moved. By this time, having seen what she was accomplishing, Archbishop Corrigan was her strongest supporter and champion. She made trips back to Europe to keep the work there going and to bring new Sisters to the United States, but for all practical purposes New York was the center of her operation. It was in New York that she founded her first hospital, again for Italian immigrants because she believed they were discriminated against in other institutions. Today Columbus Hospital is a major health-care center in crowded central New York City. By the time Columbus Hospital was founded, Mother Cabrini's community was only twelve years old with fourteen houses and two hundred nuns.

It was now time for greater international development, so Mother Cabrini began foundations in Nicaragua, Argentina, Panama, and France. Schools were added in Brooklyn, the Bronx, and New Jersey. She opened a day school and orphanage in New Orleans. In 1899 the Servite Fathers asked her to come to Chicago. She took fourteen Sisters with her and began new undertakings there. She found conditions among the poor every bit as bad as those in New York; but with the East Coast experience behind her, she did not have to experiment to tackle the new problems. Eventually she was to open Columbus Hospital in Chicago in the renovated North Shore Hotel. In acquiring this hotel she showed her sharp business sense. In the negotiations for the property the owners had committed all the land surrounding the hotel. Several days before the signing she took several Sisters and went out and measured the land. She discovered that the owners had moved the surveyor's stakes, hoping to keep some valuable land. The stakes were back in their original positions when the deed was signed.

Mother Cabrini was also a shrewd fund raiser, and the bankers who had to deal with her soon came to respect her. In Seattle, where she had become an American citizen, when she had trouble getting a loan from Christian bankers to buy the Perry Hotel for a foundling home, a Jewish banker came to her assistance. When he asked what money she needed, she led him down a corridor to a statue of St. Ann. She took a note from the hands of the statue of this good Jewish mother and handed it to the banker. It contained the amount she needed. The banker assured her that the figure would be met. Again, in New Orleans, when she wanted to build a new orphanage because the one she had was overcrowded, she called on a wealthy Italian shipowner who had only given pennies to her Sisters when they had approached him. When the man, Captain Salvatore Pizzati, inquired what she wanted, she asked if he would come to her St. Philip Street house that night to see something. He agreed. When he arrived after dusk, she led him into the dormitory where clean white beds were crowded, wall to wall. She took the shipowner to a crib where two baby girls were sleeping.

233

She informed him that each could not have her own bed because there wasn't room for another crib.

"You are a Sicilian," Mother Cabrini told the captain, "and so were their dead parents. You are named Salvatore [Savior] and they look to you to deliver them from these crowded conditions."

"Mother Cabrini, why didn't you come to me sooner and tell me about these little angels?" the old sea captain asked. "Go find land, draw up plans, and I will build you a new orphanage."

When the captain had gone, Mother Cabrini's Sisters congratulated her on her success. Mother Cabrini told them that the generous heart of the Sicilian could grow cold and others could persuade him that he was too generous. "Tomorrow I will be at his door with a lawyer's contract for him to sign. I will tell him that I will ask the Holy Father to make him a Knight of St. Gregory for his generosity," Mother Cabrini confided in her spiritual daughters. She did present the surprised captain with their agreement; he did try to back out when some liberal and anticlerical Italians told him he was too generous. Mother Cabrini held him to the contract and Pope Pius X did make the happy captain a Knight of St. Gregory.

Now it seemed as if Mother Cabrini was continually on the road. She went back and forth to Europe and Latin America to visit her nuns. Foundations were made in England and Brazil. She opened a school in Denver and sent her Sisters into the Colorado mining camps to seek out Italian workers and their families. In Los Angeles she founded a school and orphanage. She told her nuns to take particular care of the Mexican population, remarking, "Priests are so few here that the heretics have long since sowed their cockle." Los Angeles, then only a city of one hundred fifty thousand people, intrigued her — and perhaps she was the first to observe a phenomenon many others would later notice. In a letter she sent to her headquarters Mother Cabrini observed, "I have never seen a place in which there was a greater number of sects, and of the most ridiculous kind. The divine sun and the perfumed flowers seem to draw them like flies."

In 1905 the Missionary Sisters of the Sacred Heart celebrated the twenty-fifth anniversary of their foundation at Codogno. The society now numbered a thousand Sisters scattered around the world in fifty houses. Some five thousand orphans were being sheltered and many thousands of students were in schools Mother Cabrini began. The indefatigable nun was finally beginning to tire. She suffered from malarial attacks, having caught the disease on one of her journeys; moreover, her lungs had never been strong. Her favorite foundation was at West Park, for here on a hill above the Hudson River she could find peace and retirement. The first time she saw the property she said that it was there she wanted to be buried. And so in 1910 she thought it would be best for her community if she retired and allowed a younger Sister to take over. She let her spiritual daughters know that it was time for a replacement. Soon letters were flying between her houses, gathered, and sent to Rome. Pope Pius X responded to the requests of Mother Cabrini's nuns and decreed that Mother Cabrini was to remain superior general for life. So back on the road she went, founding new institutions, replacing those that had grown too small, encouraging and strengthening her Sisters.

In the spring of 1917 she arrived in Chicago from the

West Coast. Her nuns were alarmed at her paleness and weakness. Because she was on the verge of collapse, she allowed doctors to examine her. The problem was once again malaria. As spring turned to summer, she seemed to be responding to treatment, but it was only temporary. In November her weakness returned and she was more and more confined to her bed. When she could, she arose for Mass and meals and the recreation period of the Sisters. As Christmas approached, she helped plan for the feast, picking out a Christmas card to be sent and assisting in preparing candy for the children. On Friday, December 21, she attended Mass and made her adoration for the last time. The next day she was too weak to rise. Mother Antoinette, the hospital superior, came to see her; but Mother Cabrini told her she was a bit weary and would rise later. It was the last anyone would hear her speak. Some time later she got up, opened her door, and rang a bell to call her Sisters. They found her sitting in her rocking chair and as they gathered around her she died. Still to come were solemn requiem Masses in Chicago and New York, her burial at West Park, her beatification in 1938, and finally her canonization at St. Peter's on July 7, 1946, to become the first canonized citizen of the United States.

# CHAPTER 16

## *A Woman of Conscience*

### *Dorothy Day*

The first half of the twentieth century was a time for the social awakening of American Catholics. The ground had been laid by papal social encyclicals of Leo XIII and Pius XI and by such men as Father Peter Dietz, Monsignor John Ryan, and Father John Cronin. But it was a woman who gave flesh to their principles and who by her writing and actions made their teachings come alive and who was the motivating force and rallying point for young intellectual Catholics across America. The phrase "peace and justice" is a modern slogan for activism, but the woman who took these words from the abstract to a presence on the streets of America was Dorothy Day.

Dorothy Day was born in the Bath Beach section of Brooklyn on November 8, 1897. Her father, John, was a Tennesseean of Scotch-Irish ancestry who made his living as a newspaperman with a penchant for horses. Her mother, Grace, came from upstate New York. Through her parents, Dorothy was not only eligible for the Daughters of the American Revolution but also the United Daughters of the Confederacy. The family moved to the Bay area of California in time for her to survive the 1906 earthquake. The family then went to Chicago where Dorothy had most of her schooling. She graduated from high school in 1914, winning a Hearst scholarship that enabled her to enroll at the University of Illinois in Urbana where she also had to work at menial jobs to support herself. Like so many young people before her and after her, the new freedom and independence of being away from home caused her to discard old values. She rejected religion as having no relevance, read Russian writers, moved in radical circles, wrote for *The Daily Illini*, and in general kicked up her heels.

Dorothy's formal education ended after two years at Urbana. Her father obtained a new job on the *Morning Telegraph* in New York and since she did not want to be separated from her family she made the move with them. She had decided to become a journalist, like her father (although he purportedly did not approve of it), and made the rounds of the New York newspapers; however, none would take her. She finally found a position with the *New York Call*, a Socialist morning paper, and took a room on Cherry Street to be near her work. Some of her assignments were to cover radical speakers who came to New York, and she was so moved by Elizabeth Gurley Flynn's plea for miners that she gave Miss Flynn every penny she had and had to borrow money to get back to her office. She worked closely with Mike Gold, city editor of the *Call*, who later became editor of the Communist *Daily Worker*. She interviewed Leon Trotsky and covered peace marches in Washington.

When the *Call* folded because of lack of funds, she found a job as assistant editor of *The Masses*, a radical magazine that was edited by Max Eastman. She lived in Greenwich Village and was well known to the night lifers there. It was a time of revolutionary songs, little sleep, and great excitement. The end of *The Masses* came when the government removed its mailing permit and it had to close. She joined a suffragette march in Washington and for the first time (1917) was arrested and thrown in jail where she took part in a hunger strike. The warden finally announced that she and the others were pardoned by the president. They refused the pardon, saying they had done nothing wrong, but were thrown out of jail as unceremoniously as they had been thrown in. She went back to her Greenwich Village life, spent time at the Provincetown Playhouse on MacDougal Street, and hung out in a bar called The Hell Hole where she was a drinking companion to the likes of Eugene O'Neill and Maxwell Bodenheim. She wrote for the *Liberator*, a new radical-chic magazine which Max Eastman was making the voice of the Russian revolution; she also studied to be a nurse probationer and met Lionel Moise with whom she was soon living, became pregnant, allowed Moise to take her to an abortionist, and was then deserted by him. It was a period she called her "downward path to salvation."

Dorothy bounced back from the Moise affair by marrying within months a man named Barkeley Tobey who did public relations work for book publishers. Tobey had money from his family and hence did not have to work. The couple went to Europe and returned to New York in the summer of 1921, having been in London, Paris, and Rome. It was a period in her life that Dorothy did not talk about. She later summed it up to friends, according to her best biographer, William Miller, in these words: "I married a man on the rebound, after an unhappy love affair. He took me to Europe and when we got back I left him. I felt I had used him and was ashamed."

With her marriage ended, a period of aimless wandering began. Dorothy went to Chicago, was arrested in an

239

International Workers of the World lodging house, and was jailed. When she was released, she took odd jobs, worked on a book, and wrote for a Communist paper. With a friend she drifted to New Orleans's French Quarter. She found a job on the *Item*, interviewing people like Eleonora Duse and doing special reporting. Returning to New York, she renewed old friendships, among them the Malcolm Cowleys, and began a whirl of parties. Not long after her return, Dorothy bought a beach house on Staten Island, and in 1925 she entered a common-law marriage with Forster Batterham (an anarchist from an old Tennessee family who had been trained as a biologist but who avoided work by going fishing). The couple spent most of their time on Staten Island, Dorothy writing and Forster either on the beach or on a pier with a fishing pole. Dorothy became pregnant and moved back into the city to have her baby, who turned out to be a girl whom she named Tamar Teresa. When an Italian woman in the next bed heard the name "Teresa," she offered Dorothy a medal of St. Thérèse of Lisieux. "I don't believe in those things," Dorothy replied; yet, despite the brusqueness, Dorothy was beginning to think seriously of religion again. Over the years, there had been flickering thoughts of religion, but she had let them pass her by. Now she wondered if she should have the baby baptized but typically did nothing about it. The seeds were there, but the ground was still sterile.

It was Tamar who wrought the change. For the first time Dorothy had accepted responsibility for someone else. "I did not want my child to flounder as I had so often floundered," she wrote later. Her child would need religious roots. Although her work had taken her into some churches, she said in one of her books that it was only in a Catholic church that she had felt the presence of God. Again her thoughts turned to baptism for her child. She talked the matter over with Forster, who accused her of "morbid escapism"; but the thought would not go away. Near the beach cottage was St. Joseph's Home, an institution run by the Sisters of Charity for unwed mothers and illegitimate babies. Wheeling Tamar past the building one day, Dorothy met Sister Aloysia, an elderly but feisty nun who had taught school for many years and was now semi-retired to care for babies. She told the nun that she would like to have her child baptized, and from then on Sister Aloysia took over.

It was not a simple matter. Sister talked to a priest who said that he had to be sure Tamar would be raised as a Catholic. This meant that Dorothy would have to know her child's faith. Sister gave Dorothy a catechism and the two of them went to work. Dorothy began going to Mass at the Sisters' chapel and saying the rosary. Tamar was baptized, much to Forster's displeasure. Dorothy knew that she would have to follow her daughter into the Church, and her growing religiosity angered Forster who was jealous of her new interest. He left her a number of times only to come back. Finally, Dorothy took a stand and told him that the relationship was over. With the decision made she arranged to be baptized. The ceremony took place on December 28, 1927, and Sister Aloysia was her sponsor. After the baptism she made her first confession and the next day received her first Holy Communion. She was to say years later that she never regretted for one minute the step she had taken.

Back in the city she summarized novels that had

screen possibilities for MGM and did public relations for the Anti-Imperialist League, a Communist front formed to support Augusto Sandino in Nicaragua and oppose U.S. military intervention there. She found a spiritual director who was not put off by her radical interests. A prolific reader, she now began to devour Catholic books. Pathé Films offered her a contract to write dialogue for movies and she went to Hollywood with Tamar where she was given little to do. She was not surprised when the contract was not renewed. She then went to Mexico where the Church was being persecuted and supported herself writing articles for *Commonweal*, a Catholic intellectual journal. Later she would also write for *America* and *Jubilee*, but these Catholic publications paid poorly and she went back to Staten Island for the summer and to her mother in Florida for the winter. In New York she found an apartment on East Twelfth Street, among the poor whom she loved so much, and on the same street was Our Lady, Help of Christians, her new church. Coming back to New York from a "hunger march" on Washington, D.C., she found a man waiting for her at her apartment; this encounter at the end of 1932 was to change her life forever. The man was Peter Maurin — and someone more fastidious than Dorothy, one who could not see through poverty to true quality, might have summarily dismissed him. It was providential that Dorothy should not.

Peter was twenty years older than Dorothy, a peasant from southern France. He had gone to a Christian Brothers' school in Paris and then taught there. He went to Canada to homestead, but after his partner died he took odd jobs until he entered the United States in 1911. Although he was primarily interested in the land and man's relationship to the land, to survive he had to work in steel mills, railroad yards, brickyards, and every kind of place imaginable. He had been jailed for vagrancy and for the preceding seven years had been living and working at a Catholic boys' camp in the Catskills. He had become acquainted with George Shuster, then editor of *Commonweal*; and Shuster, knowing Dorothy's Socialist and Communist background, had recommended him to her. Peter had an idea for a Catholic labor paper and Shuster thought Dorothy might be interested.

Dorothy, as it turned out, was interested. Her publishing background and her writing made a paper appealing, but first Peter said she needed some additional formation. He set her on a task of reading: Father Vincent McNabb, Eric Gill, Jacques Maritain, Léon Bloy, Charles Péguy, Luigi Sturzo, Karl Adam, and Nikolai Berdyaev. He recommended books of history and lives of the saints. Beyond reading, Peter himself was a great teacher. It could have remained all talk, but that was not Peter's way. He was an activist and he revealed a plan that he had probably thought over many times. While the paper would focus attention on the movement, its purpose would be to give answers to the unemployment of the times (the Great Depression was on) by promoting communal living and a return to the land. There would be houses of hospitality that would be centers for lectures and discussions. Farming communes would introduce the needy to the land. Peter had the ideas and it would fall to Dorothy to carry them out. Peter wanted to call the paper *The Catholic Radical*, but Dorothy decided on *The Catholic Worker*. It was a wise choice, as the paper would be a Catholic response to the Communist *Daily Worker*; of equal importance, the term "radical" might frighten some off, while almost everyone could identify with workers.

Dorothy learned that the Paulist Press would print twenty-five thousand copies of an eight-page tabloid for fifty-seven dollars. But where would the money come from? It was a problem that would be with Dorothy for the rest of her life. A Newark pastor contributed ten dollars. A nun Dorothy met gave her a dollar. She was owed for an article in *The Sign* and she had some money coming for some research she did for a Paulist Father. So at the worst of times — the height of the Depression — Dorothy launched the paper in time for May Day, 1933, and she and some helpers rushed to Union Square to sell copies to participants in the Communist rally. (The paper was offered at a penny a copy, and still is today.) The publication became the voice of the movement, with Peter contributing the theory in one of his "Easy Essays" (a sort of blank-verse rationalization), and Dorothy expounding the practice in her column which went through several titles before she settled for "On Pilgrimage."

The paper found ready acceptance, not among Communists but with college students and seminarians, as well as many priests and concerned laity. Thousands who had never heard of Dorothy Day or Peter Maurin eagerly looked forward to the monthly columns. Although printed on newsprint, both the writing and artwork that appeared in the publication showed much quality. The circulation grew rapidly — twenty thousand by September and then a hundred thousand. The paper attracted young people who wanted to work with Dorothy, and the first "house of hospitality" came into existence. There were moves to larger and larger quarters: to Charles Street and then to two large houses on Mott Street which became headquarters for the movement; and it was through Dorothy's begging that all this was supported. Peter had begun his lectures, and with each lecture more and more people came to listen to him. Some of the leading Catholic thinkers of New York came to speak at the nightly meetings — among them Carlton Hayes, John La Farge, Parker Moon, and Wilfrid Parsons. Visitors such as Jacques Maritain and Hilaire Belloc made sure that their visits to New York included a stop at Mott Street. Dorothy had become widely known in Catholic circles, and there were more and more invitations coming in for her to lecture.

What Dorothy had done was hit a raw nerve among concerned Catholics. She took the dry bones of abstract texts on economics and sociology, the obtuse language of papal encyclicals, the general do-goodism of Sunday sermons, and put flesh on them all. She made poverty and injustice come alive by personal examples, causing her readers to become involved. Her teachings formed a generation of concerned seminarians, and through them affected the Church all over the United States. Where Dorothy once stood alone, today many other Catholic publications have followed.

I can think of no one who had more influence on today's Catholic social conscience than Dorothy Day in *The Catholic Worker*, which attacked head-on the problems of the time: poverty, unemployment, racism, the unjust distribution of goods, the destruction of our environment — all subjects taken for granted today but with little general Catholic awareness before Dorothy Day. What was surprising was that Dorothy's acceptance went across the Catholic spectrum. The first gift to *The Catholic Worker* came from Pat Scanlan, the very conservative editor of *The Tablet* of Brooklyn. Scanlan also publicized the work in his paper. Later he would oppose her.

The change came because of Dorothy's total commitment to pacifism. She never shied away from unpopular causes and was an opponent of racism, both against blacks and Jews. She had championed the Scottsboro youths — nine Alabama blacks accused of raping two white women — when the only others defending them seemed to be Communists. It was her pacifism that brought the first hostility to the movement. Because of her principles, Dorothy declared that *The Catholic Worker* was neutral in the Spanish Civil War; to the Catholic right this seemed like heresy, and the right began to insinuate that perhaps she was a Communist. Her antiwar stance led her to oppose World War II and the Korean and Vietnamese wars. The paper not only supported conscientious objection to those wars but urged this position on its readers. Dorothy also strongly opposed the atomic bomb. In the early days after World War II when there were air-raid drills, Dorothy refused to take shelter and was arrested. Her position on these matters caused her to lose support; but at the same time she attracted others like Ammon Hennacy, and she was the forerunner of people like Father Daniel Berrigan who took their inspiration from her example. Through all these difficult years she proved that where her principles were concerned, there could be no compromise. War was opposed to the teaching of Christ, *period*. In the patriotic fervor of World War II many had deserted her, and she observed later that during this period about eighty percent of her young Catholic Workers had "betrayed" her pacifist ideals.

The major support for her work came through the paper, but it was a hand-to-mouth existence. Her column more than once recorded something like "Telephone turned off; gas and electricity next." She supplemented the donations the paper brought in by constant traveling and lecturing. She had to work even harder because of the war in Europe. She wrote that in 1938, "thanks to the thirty Houses of Hospitality over the country, and widespread circulation in many schools and colleges, we had a regular run of 160,000 copies a month. Since the war, and our pacifist stand, our circulation has dropped to 50,000." But she believed that what was left provided stronger support. She visited these other houses, spoke at colleges and seminaries, called on formers of Catholic opinion. Her peregrinations and promotions, her dreams and aspirations, her difficulties and her successes — all of these were recorded by her. Her books are the prime source for any biographer: *From Union Square to Rome* (1938), *On Pilgrimage* (1948), *The Long Loneliness* (1952).

So the years passed. Dorothy's daughter, Tamar, grew up and married, eventually making Dorothy a grandmother many times over. Peter Maurin's last years were sad, as his mind retreated to infancy (until a few years ago called senility but which would now be diagnosed as Alzheimer's disease). He died on May 15, 1949, and was buried from Transfiguration Church on Mott Street in a Brooklyn cemetery plot donated by a Dominican priest. Age too was beginning to slow Dorothy. Her religious practices, always fervent, became even more so. During the 1960s when many priests and Sisters were deserting their vocations, some of them sought to become part of one of her houses or farms. She discouraged them by telling them that "faithfulness and perseverance are the greatest of virtues." She explained that in a short time they would become disillusioned with the Catholic Worker movement and they would move on to something else: "It is the usual pattern, and I know how little peace there is in it." She was getting about now with a cane, ailing from rheumatism and arthritis. An unexpected heart attack, suffered after talking on peace at the 1976 Eucharistic Congress in Philadelphia, made her a semi-invalid. Her traveling was over, and her contacts now came about through correspondence. More time was given to her daily devotions — Mass; recitation of the psalms and rosary; meditation and reading. She continued her "On Pilgrimage" columns, but as her biographer William Miller observes, they "became a litany of death," surviving old friends and co-workers whose passing she recorded.

Dorothy Day died quietly in the early morning of November 28, 1980, three weeks after celebrating her eighty-third birthday. Only her daughter, Tamar, was with her. Her grandchildren escorted the pine box that was her burial shroud into Transfiguration Church. The people of the area whom she had assisted so many times were her mourners. Cardinal Terence Cooke presided. Since her death, some who knew her and some who were inspired by her have been promoting her cause for sainthood. What develops from that is in God's hands; however, her struggles for justice and peace by restoring all things in Christ will be an inspiration for many yet unborn; they may not even recognize the name Dorothy Day but her influence will go on like concentric circles down through time.

My own memory of her is best served in a picture

taken in 1973 that appeared in newspapers across the United States. It shows an old woman in a dowdy dress, wearing a large floppy straw hat to keep the California sun off her and carrying a cane, being led away by a policeman after having been arrested for marching with Cesar Chavez's United Farm Workers. There is a dignity in the woman and a determination in her step. It is typical Dorothy Day, never fearful of putting her beliefs into action whatever the consequences.

# Index of People

Adam, Karl — 243
Adams, John — 48
Adams, John Quincy — 178
Altham, John — 44

Babade, Pierre — 213f
Badin, Francis Vincent — 112
Badin, Stephen Theodore — 65, 108, 110ff, 144
Barat, Madeleine Sophie — 219, 221
Batterham, Forster — 240f
Bayley, James Roosevelt — 141, 189f
Belloc, Hilaire — 245
Benedict XV — 204
Bent, Charles — 160
Berdyaev, Nikolai — 243
Berrigan, Daniel — 246
Berry, Luke — 131
Blanc, Anthony — 108
Blanchet, Francis N. — 33
Bloy, Léon — 243
Bodenheim, Maxwell — 239
Boyer, Jean Pierre — 180
Brébeuf, John de — 1
Brownson, Orestes — 191, 193
Bruté, Simon — 108, 120, 125ff, 130, 137ff, 216f
Bucareli y Ursúa, Antonio María — 80f

Cabeza de Vaca, Álvar Núñez — 14
Cabrini, Frances Xavier — 225ff

Calvert, Cecil — 44
Calvert, George — 44
Calvert, Leonard — 44
Carroll, Charles (of Carrollton) — 43ff, 130, 142
Carroll, Daniel (of Rock Creek) — 43ff
Carroll, John — 43ff, 111, 121, 124f, 139, 141, 212f, 216
Carson, Kit — 160
Cather, Willa — 148, 156
Chabanel, Noël — 1
Charles I — 44
Chase, Samuel — 47, 57
Chavez, Cesar — 250
Cheverus, John — 65, 141, 213
Clement XIV — 73
Columbus, Christopher — 14f
Concanen, Richard Luke — 65
Connolly, John — 128, 131
Cooke, Terence — 248
Cornwallis, Charles — 107
Coronado, Francisco Vásquez de — 1
Corrigan, Michael — 194, 229ff
Couture, William — 5f
Cowley, Malcolm — 240
Crespi, Juan — 77f
Cronin, John — 237

Daniel, Anthony — 1
Darnall, Henry — 43, 45
David, John — 108, 111
Day, Dorothy — 237ff
Day, Tamar Teresa — 240ff, 247f
De Grasse, François — 107

De Smet, Jean Pierre — 2, 27ff, 152f, 155, 218, 221
De Soto, Hernando — 14
Dietz, Peter — 237
Drexel, Katherine — 207
Dubois, John — 63, 118ff, 140, 214
Dubourg, Louis William — 64, 124, 213f, 219f
Duchesne, Rose Philippine — 218ff
Duse, Eleonora — 240

Eagle Woman — 36f
Eastman, Max — 238
Eccleston, Samuel — 135
Egan, Michael — 65
Elliott, Walter — 199
England, John — 128, 168ff

Fages, Pedro — 78ff, 87
Falconio, Diomede — 99
Farley, John — 100, 102, 204
Fenwick, Benedict — 128f, 170
Fenwick, Edward — 111
Filicchi, Antonio — 64, 211, 217
Fitzgerald, Edward — 188
FitzSimons, Thomas — 60
Flaget, Benedict — 65, 108, 110ff, 139ff, 143, 149f
Flynn, Elizabeth Gurley — 238
Ford, Francis X. — 103f
Fournier, Michael — 111
Francis Joseph I — 203
Francis of Assisi — 71
Francis Xavier — 3, 144, 227
Franklin, Benjamin — 47, 57ff, 198

Frémont, John C. — 161
Frontenac, Louis de Buade, Comte de Palluau et de — 17,
  21f

Gall — 39
Gallegos, José — 156
Gallitzen, Demetrius Augustine — 41
Galpin, Charles E. — 36f
Garnier, Charles — 1
Gaston, William — 142, 176, 178
Gibbons, James — 90, 93, 99ff, 183ff
Gill, Eric — 243
Gold, Michael — 238
Goupil, René — 1, 5ff
Gregory XVI — 180

Harney, William S. — 34f
Hawthorne, Nathaniel — 189, 207
Hayes, Carlton — 245
Healy, James — 194
Hecker, Isaac — 191, 199f
Hennacy, Ammon — 246
Henrietta Maria — 44
Henry, Patrick — 121
Hoban, Michael — 103
Hughes, John — 125, 134f

Ireland, John — 195, 199, 201f

Jefferson, Thomas — 48, 60
Jogues, Isaac — 1ff
John Baptist de la Salle — 16
Johnson, Andrew — 186
Jolliet, Louis — 15, 18, 22ff

Keane, John — 195
Kenrick, Francis — 136, 184f
Kino, Eusebio — 41

LaBarge, Joseph — 36, 39
La Farge, John — 245
Lafayette, Marie Joseph Paul Yves Roch Gilbert du Motier
    [Marquis de Lafayette] — 107, 119f
Lalande, John — 1, 12f
Lalemant, Gabriel — 1
Lamy, John — 41, 148ff
Lathrop, Rose Hawthorne — 189, 207
Layton, Mary — 220
Lee, Charles — 57
L'Enfant, Pierre — 52
Leo XIII — 191f, 196, 201, 229, 237
Levins, Thomas — 131ff
Lewis, John — 58f
Lynch, Dominick — 60

Machebeuf, Joseph — 148ff
Madison, James — 65
Manning, Henry — 195
Maréchal, Ambrose — 126, 128ff, 169ff
Margil, Antonio — 41
Maritain, Jacques — 243, 245
Marquette, Jacques — 2, 14ff
Martínez, Antonio — 159f
Matignon, Francis — 213
Maurin, Peter — 242ff, 247
McCloskey, John — 125, 202
McGill, John — 189
NcNabb, Vincent — 243

Meyer, Bernard — 103
Miège, John — 161
Miki, Paul — 3
Moise, Lionel — 239
Monroe, James — 120f, 178
Montmagny, Charles de — 10
Moon, Parker — 245

Nagot, Charles — 62
Napoleon Bonaparte — 139, 219, 227
Neale, Leonard — 65, 67
Nerinckx, Charles — 27f, 65, 111
Neumann, John N. — 152
Noll, John — 95

O'Brien, Matthew — 212
O'Connell, Daniel — 169
O'Connell, William — 91, 100
O'Neill, Eugene — 239
Otrihoure — 12

Paca, William — 47
Padilla, Juan de — 1
Palou, Francisco — 71, 73ff
Parsons, Wilfrid — 245
Paul VI — 217
Péguy, Charles — 243
Pike, Zebulon — 161
Pius VI — 60, 63
Pius VII — 170
Pius IX — 188, 198
Pius X — 203, 234f
Pius XI — 13, 237

Pizzati, Salvatore — 233f
Plunkett, Robert — 60
Pokagon — 113
Portolá, Gasparde — 76f
Poulton, Thomas — 54
Powderly, Terence — 194
Power, John — 128ff
Price, Thomas Frederick — 89ff, 187
Purcell, John — 116f, 125, 134f, 149f, 163

Rampolla del Tindaro, Mariano — 202f
Raverdy, John — 162, 164
Richard, Gabriel — 41, 108, 113, 175
Richelieu, Armand Jean du Plessis, duc de [Cardinal
    Richelieu] — 1
Robespierre, Maximilien — 118ff
Rochambeau, Jean de — 107
Rockefeller, John D. — 103
Roosevelt, Franklin Delano — 189
Roosevelt, Theodore — 203
Rose of Lima — 218
Rossiter, John — 1
Ryan, John — 237

St. Vrain, Ceran — 160
Salmon, Anthony — 111
Sandino, Augusto — 242
Scalabrini, Giovanni — 229, 231
Scanlan, Patrick — 246
Serra, Junípero — 68ff
Serrati, Antonio — 226f
Seton, Elizabeth Ann Bayley — 64, 67, 124, 126, 135,
    141f, 176, 189, 209ff

Seton, William Magee — 210f
Shuster, George — 243
Sitting Bull — 35ff
Sorin, Edward — 117
Soubirous, Bernadette — 102
Spalding, Martin J. — 185ff
Sturzo, Luigi — 243

Tabb, John Bannister — 190
Taft, William H. — 203
Taney, Roger Brooke — 121
Tertullian — 1
Thérèse of Lisieux — 240
Tisserant, John — 213
Tobey, Barkeley — 239
Toussaint, Pierre — 131
Trotsky, Leon — 238

Urban VIII — 9

Vest, George — 31
Vizcaíno, Sebastián — 77f

Walsh, James Anthony — 96ff, 187
Walsh, James Edward — 103f
Washington, George — 50, 63, 107
Weld, Thomas — 61
White, Andrew — 44
White, Edward — 203
Whitfield, James — 173
Wilson, Woodrow — 204